# PRESIDENTS OF THE U.S.A.

# BUILDERS OF THE REPUBLIC

GEORGE WASHINGTON . . . . . . . . . . . . . . 16
JOHN ADAMS . . . . . . . . . . . . . . . . . . . 28
THOMAS JEFFERSON . . . . . . . . . . . . . . . 32
JAMES MADISON . . . . . . . . . . . . . . . . . 38
JAMES MONROE . . . . . . . . . . . . . . . . . . 44
JOHN QUINCY ADAMS. . . . . . . . . . . . . . . 48

# DEMOCRACY ON TRIAL

ANDREW JACKSON . . . . . . . . . . . . . . . . . 56
MARTIN VAN BUREN . . . . . . . . . . . . . . . 66
WILLIAM HENRY HARRISON . . . . . . . . . . . 70
JOHN TYLER . . . . . . . . . . . . . . . . . . . . 72
JAMES K. POLK. . . . . . . . . . . . . . . . . . . 74
ZACHARY TAYLOR . . . . . . . . . . . . . . . . . 76
MILLARD FILLMORE. . . . . . . . . . . . . . . . 80
FRANKLIN PIERCE . . . . . . . . . . . . . . . . 82
JAMES BUCHANAN . . . . . . . . . . . . . . . . 84

# CIVIL WAR & RECONSTRUCTION

ABRAHAM LINCOLN . . . . . . . . . . . . . . . . 88
ANDREW JOHNSON. . . . . . . . . . . . . . . . . 106
ULYSSES S. GRANT . . . . . . . . . . . . . . . . 110
RUTHERFORD B. HAYES. . . . . . . . . . . . . . 118
JAMES A. GARFIELD . . . . . . . . . . . . . . . 120
CHESTER A. ARTHUR. . . . . . . . . . . . . . . 122
GROVER CLEVELAND. . . . . . . . . . . . . . . 124
BENJAMIN HARRISON . . . . . . . . . . . . . . 130
WILLIAM MCKINLEY . . . . . . . . . . . . . . . 132

# TWENTIETH CENTURY LEADERS

THEODORE ROOSEVELT . . . . . . . . . . . . . 138
WILLIAM HOWARD TAFT . . . . . . . . . . . . 150
WOODROW WILSON . . . . . . . . . . . . . . . 154
WARREN G. HARDING . . . . . . . . . . . . . . 164
CALVIN COOLIDGE. . . . . . . . . . . . . . . . . 166
HERBERT HOOVER . . . . . . . . . . . . . . . . 170
FRANKLIN DELANO ROOSEVELT . . . . . . . 174
HARRY S. TRUMAN. . . . . . . . . . . . . . . . 186
DWIGHT D. EISENHOWER . . . . . . . . . . . . 192
JOHN F. KENNEDY . . . . . . . . . . . . . . . . 200

Presidential Elections 1789-1960. . . . . . . . 210
Acknowledgments . . . . . . . . . . . . . . . . . 214

# INTRODUCTION

# PROFILES AND PICTURES

## BY CORNEL LENGYEL

DEDICATION

To Raffaele and Giulia Buonocore

in appreciation . . .

# CONTENTS

Since Washington's first term the Presidency has developed into the most challenging, most burdensome, most splendid office in the western world. Chosen by a free people in free elections, the President of the United States today wields more power than any Pharaoh or Caesar ever did. Pledged to uphold the revolutionary ideas of the nation's founders, he is elected to preserve, protect and defend the world's first and longest enduring democracy, "conceived in liberty and dedicated to the proposition that all men are created equal." His words and acts can affect the lives of all the earth's inhabitants.

Though his duties in general are prescribed by the Constitution, his powers have increased with the growth of the country, developments in science and technology, and through examples set by men who have held the office. In the interval of 172 years between President Washington's inauguration in 1789 and President Kennedy's inauguration in 1961, the United States developed from a small agricultural country into the most productive industrial nation on earth. The thirteen colonies which fought for independence in 1776 had less than 4,000,000 inhabitants. Today the fifty states of the Union have more than 180,000,000 citizens. And in area the United States has increased from 323,000 square miles to 3,628,000 square miles.

When Washington was elected, he was the first and only President in a world ruled by hereditary monarchs. Since then, America's example has had a liberating effect on countries in every portion of the globe. Washington's first budget covered but a single handwritten sheet of paper. The national budget for 1960-61 is more than 1200 printed pages. During Washington's administration there were 2000 federal employees. In 1960 there were more than 2,400,000. President Washington had less than a dozen newspapers to consult for clues to public opinion. President Kennedy consults a daily digest of 750 newspapers; his press conferences are attended by more than 500 reporters; his television broadcasts are heard and seen by 70,000,000 people.

To prevent too much power from accruing to any one person or group of persons in government, the Founding Fathers put certain safeguards into the Constitution, which remains one of the clearest and most effective blueprints for the government of a free people. They devised a system of checks and balances to control the legislative, the executive, and the judicial departments. The President's office is defined in Article II, second among the seven short articles which make up the Constitution. It states the way in which the President is to be elected, his qualifications, oath, term and salary. It lists his specific powers, including the power to make treaties and appointments "by and with the advice and consent of the Senate." It indicates how and why the President may be impeached and removed from office.

Despite the limitations on his power, there were fears in the beginning that the President might turn himself into a dictator. Patrick Henry called the Presidency "that awful squint toward monarchy." Jefferson remarked: "Sometimes it is said that man cannot be trusted with the government of himself. Can he then be trusted with the government of others? Or have we found angels in the form of kings to govern him?" When Andrew Jackson was elected, Henry Clay complained: "We are in the midst of a revolution rapidly tending towards the concentration of all power in the hands of one man . . ." A century later N. J. Small wrote: "Nothing is more evident in the history of the Presidency than the steady accumulation of power in that office." Another historian, Henry Jones Ford, observed: "Since Jackson's time American democracy has revived the oldest political institution of the race: elective kingship."

Elected to serve a term of four years as the country's Chief Executive, Chief Diplomat, and Commander-in-Chief, the President is not only chief of his party: he is chief representative of *all* the people. Matching his powers, he has duties and responsibilities that are correspondingly great. President Washington complained that he had no leisure to read or answer the letters that were pouring in on him from all quarters. President John Adams reported: "A peck of troubles in a large bundle of papers, often in a handwriting almost illegible, comes every day." Jefferson called his office "a splendid misery." Woodrow Wilson declared: "The President is the most heavily burdened officer in the world. No other man's day is so filled as his, so full of respon-

sibilities which tax mind and conscience alike and demand an inexhaustible vitality." Truman said, "The job is almost fantastic. No man can really fill the Presidency. The Presidency has too many and too great responsibilities. All a man can do is to try to meet them." The job is big, as big as the man who fills it. A strong President will exert moral leadership and leave his mark on the times. A mediocre President will mark time, raise dust, or let party leaders run the government.

Who are the men who have held the highest office and how do they rank as Presidents? In a 1948 poll, Arthur M. Schlesinger, Sr., professor of history at Harvard, asked 55 authorities to rate the performance of the Presidents. The survey did not cover President Truman, then in office, nor Presidents William Henry Harrison and James Garfield, whose terms were cut short by death. The results of the poll:

I. GREAT: Lincoln, Washington, Franklin Roosevelt, Jefferson, Wilson, Jackson (in order of preference).

II. NEAR GREAT: John Adams, Polk, Cleveland, Theodore Roosevelt.

III. AVERAGE: Madison, Monroe, John Quincy Adams, Van Buren, Hayes, Johnson, Taft, McKinley, Benjamin Harrison, Hoover.

IV. BELOW AVERAGE: Tyler, Fillmore, Taylor, Buchanan, Pierce, Coolidge.

V. FAILURE: Grant, Harding.

Lincoln was voted first unanimously.

Of the 34 men who have been elected

Presidents, 24 were college graduates; 24, lawyers; 20, members of Congress; 17, residents of Virginia, Ohio, or New York; 13, governors of their states; 13, members of Phi Beta Kappa; 12, generals in the U.S. Army. In addition to lawyers and generals, the roster includes an inventor, a railsplitter, a journeyman tailor, a professor of Greek and Latin, a rancher, an editor, a haberdasher, an engineer, a multimillionaire, a U.S. Navy veteran. The oldest was elected at the age of 68; the youngest at 43.

The lives of the Presidents, however brief, are a vital part of the American saga. Their profiles present the changing profile of democratic man. By and large the people's choice, they mirror the hopes and aspirations as well as the follies and frustrations of the electorate at any given time. They reflect the many-faceted story of democracy. "A page of history is worth a volume of logic," said Oliver Wendell Holmes; while Emerson observed: "There is properly no History. Only Biography . . ."

A young visitor from Paris surveyed conditions in the United States during Andrew Jackson's administration. Returning home, he published his book of penetrating observations in 1835, *Democracy in America*. "In America I saw more than America," wrote de Tocqueville. "I saw there the image of democracy itself . . . Can it be believed that the democracy which has overthrown the feudal system and vanquished kings will retreat? . . . The advent of democracy as a governing power in the world's affairs,

universal and irresistible, is at hand." At the same time, de Tocqueville felt that the American President was too often at the mercy of Congress, which could disregard his proposals, reject his nominations, overrule his vetoes. De Tocqueville also wondered whether democratic society, with its emphasis on the equality of men, could foster the development of great or uncommon men and draw them into public service.

Since de Tocqueville's visit, the democratic process has produced and elevated to the highest office such men as Lincoln, Wilson, Franklin Roosevelt. In an office that demands remarkable capacities, less than a third of the elected men have been judged below average. A third have apparently demonstrated greatness or near-greatness. No hereditary dynasty can approach the record.

A contemporary historian, Holman Hamilton has stated: "To understand the Presidency of the future, we must understand the Presidency of the past . . . Now more than ever before, the survival of American and western civilization hinges on the American Presidency." A year before his election in 1960, John F. Kennedy remarked in an informal interview: "The job of the next President will be the hardest since Roosevelt, and I think that Roosevelt had the hardest of all except Lincoln and perhaps Washington . . . The real dilemma we face is whether a free society can compete over a long period of time with a totalitarian society in which both the carrot and the stick are used to force all human and material resources into the service of the state."

Kennedy also observed: "The next year, the next decade, in all likelihood the next generation, will require more wisdom and bravery on our part than any period in our history . . ." The 35th and youngest President of the United States is aware of the challenges that surround the island of the free world in an encroaching sea of totalitarianism. "Man holds in his mortal hands the power to abolish all forms of human poverty and all forms of human life," he stated in his inaugural in 1961.

Despite the awesome new dangers that confront democracy, the fact that men of extraordinary abilities have been elected to the Presidency—in every generation since the founding of the Republic—testifies to the abiding vitality of the democratic experiment.

—Cornel Lengyel

# BUILDERS OF THE REPUBLIC

*Even if the clouds of barbarism and despotism should again obscure the science and liberties of Europe, this country remains to preserve and restore light and liberty to them. The flames kindled on July 4, 1776 have spread over too much of the globe to be extinguished . . .*

—Thomas Jefferson

scorned the young colonial's counsel. Trapped in an ambush on the banks of the Monongahela, Braddock's troops were nearly wiped out in July, 1755. Braddock was killed. Two horses were shot under Washington, four bullets passed through his coat. Plunging into the forest, he barely escaped with his life.

At twenty-seven, Washington married Martha Dandridge Custis, a rich young widow with two children. Managing his farms and woodlands, he became one of the best farmers in the country. After 1770, he became more prominent in the resistance movement. When the port of Boston was closed by George III in an effort to punish and starve the rebels, Washington said, "I will raise a thousand men at my own expense and ride to the relief of Boston."

He attended the great protest meeting in Philadelphia in the spring of 1775. While his fellow delegates in the Continental Congress were still drafting humble petitions, Washington appeared in his colonel's uniform of the Virginia militia, which was his way of saying, "We must be ready to fight for our rights." When John Adams urged his nomination and when the delegates elected him unanimously to command the people's army, forty-three-year-old Washington thanked them for the great honor; he would serve without pay, he said, but was anxious to forewarn them: "I do not think myself equal to the command I am honored with." The same evening, visiting Patrick Henry, he told the delegate with tears in his eyes, "Mark my words, Mr. Henry. From the day I enter upon command of the American armies, I date the fall and ruin of my reputation."

On his way north he learned of the battle at Bunker Hill. "Did the militia fight?" he asked. "Yes!" "Then the liberties of the country are safe," said Washington. On July 3, 1775 he took command of the camp at Cambridge. He raised the siege of Boston. A week before the Declaration of Independence was adopted, he spoke to his ragged troops of farm boys in the port of New York. Within sight of the royal armada of five hundred warships—the largest expeditionary force ever sent out to crush a people's rebellion—Washington declared: "The time is now near at hand which must probably determine whether Americans are to be free men or slaves. The fate of unborn millions will now depend upon the courage and conduct of this army. . . . Let us rely upon the goodness of the cause . . . to animate and encourage us to great and noble actions."

For seven long and bitter years, against the most unequal odds, against cold and starvation, neglect and treachery, General Washington held together a remnant of the people's army. From Valley Forge to Yorktown, his indomitable will and character preserved a nearly lost cause, a cause he had pledged himself to uphold.

After many grim reversals he finally forced Cornwallis to surrender at Yorktown on October 19, 1781. With the

help of the French Fleet the American rebellion had become a successful revolution: the people of the colonies had won the right to form a government of their own choosing. Bidding farewell to arms, Washington returned to his long-neglected farms by the Potomac.

But he could not enjoy Mount Vernon for long. In May, 1787, delegates from the thirteen newly independent and nearly sovereign states met in Philadelphia to draft a new and more effective constitution than the Articles of Confederation. Washington was asked to preside over the Constitutional Convention. After the Constitution was hammered out, the delegates elected Washington unanimously as the new nation's first President.

Some wanted to crown him King of America, but Washington dismissed the tempters with scorn. "If you have any regard for your country or respect for me, banish such thoughts forever!" Some wanted to address him with the resounding title, "His Most Gracious Highness, President of the United States and Protector of Their Liberties." The accepted title became "Mr. President."

Washington took his oath of office on April 30, 1789 at City Hall in New York, the temporary capital. "I do solemnly swear that I will faithfully execute the office of the President of the United States and will, to the best of my ability, preserve, protect and defend the Constitution of the United States."

In his inaugural address Washington spoke of America's mission. "The preser-

*After four years of retirement at Mount Vernon, General Washington presided over the Constitutional Convention, which met on May 14, 1787 to devise a new code of laws for the Union.*

24

After weeks of debate, Washington re-
minded his colleagues of the great object
before them. "Let us raise a standard to
which the wise and honest can repair.
The event is in the hands of God."

vation of the sacred fire of liberty and the destiny of the republican model of government are . . . staked on the experiment entrusted to the hands of the American people." In office, he did all he could to unify the country, to give strength and dignity to democratic government, both at home and abroad; he set the first high example in governing a free people.

Having served two terms, he refused a third. He considered it dangerous to keep any one man in power too long. In his Farewell Address, which is read in Congress each year, he gave his best parting counsel to the nation he had helped to found.

"My first wish is to see this plague of mankind—war—banished from the earth." He urged the people "to guard against the impostures of pretended patriotism. . . . Observe good faith and justice toward all nations, cultivate peace and harmony with all . . . Steer clear of permanent alliances with any portion of the foreign world . . ."

*Summary:* WASHINGTON, GEORGE. *Born: February 22, 1732 near Fredericksburg, Virginia. Died: December 14, 1799 at Mount Vernon, Virginia. Parents: Augustine Washington and Mary Ball. Education: common school. Married: Martha Custis in 1759; two step-children. Career: surveyor, farmer; officer French and Indian War, 1752-53; member, Virginia House of Burgesses, 1758-75; delegate, Continental Congress, 1774-75; Commander-in-Chief, Continental Army, 1775-83; President, Constitutional Convention, 1787: First President, 1789-97.*

# JOHN ADAMS

*Architect of the Revolution*

Son of a yeoman farmer, he left the village of Braintree at sixteen to enter Harvard College. At the time Harvard had six teachers and thirty students. Young Adams was undecided whether to become a surgeon or a clergyman. A short stocky lad, he took part in school readings of Shakespeare and was admired for his dramatic rendering of speeches from *Coriolanus*. He delivered his commencement oration in Latin, a feat which won for him his first job: teaching Latin in Worcester's one-room schoolhouse.

While teaching, he studied law and was admitted to the Boston bar in 1758. A successful attorney, he was offered high and profitable posts by the Crown. But Adams turned them down. Opposed to the oppressive acts of the royal government, he became a leader of the independence movement. Soon after the Boston Tea Party, when the port was blockaded by the Royal Navy, he left for Philadelphia to take part in the Continental Congress, the forbidden first parliament of America.

In Congress he sat on more committees and did more work than any other delegate. The bold measures he proposed to pave the way to independence alarmed or offended many of his colleagues. Adams insisted that Jefferson be the one to write a draft of the Declaration of Independence.

Adams fought for the adoption of the

Declaration, "for every word of it," and became known as the Colossus of the Debates, the Atlas of Independence.

Sent to France by Congress in 1778, Adams negotiated loans for the hard-pressed colonies. After the war he negotiated the Treaty of Peace with Great Britain. Returning home, he served as Vice-President for two terms. In 1796 he was elected President.

An honest, brilliant, crotchety nonconformist, he was soon at odds with his Cabinet, his party, with Hamilton and Jefferson. The excesses of the French Revolution horrified him; he feared the tyranny of both the majority and the minority. He did everything to prevent America from joining England in a war against France. For his future epitaph he composed the line: "Here lies John Adams, who took upon himself the responsibility of the peace with France, in the year 1800."

Failing to be re-elected, he retired to his farm at Braintree. On July 4, 1826, at the age of ninety, he died.

*Summary:* ADAMS, JOHN. *Born: October 30, 1735 at Braintree, Massachusetts. Died: July 4, 1826 at Quincy, Massachusetts. Education: Harvard, 1755. Married: Abigail Smith, 1759; five children. Career: lawyer; member of Congress, 1774-77; minister to France, 1778, and England, 1785; Vice-President, 1789-96; Second President, 1797-1801.*

*Brilliant and devoted wife of John Adams and mother of the Sixth President, Abigail Adams was the First Lady to occupy the unfinished White House.*

# THOMAS JEFFERSON

*Apostle of Democracy*

"I have sworn, upon the altar of God. eternal hostility against any form of tyranny over the mind of man." This was the theme that governed his lifelong battle in the cause of human freedom.

At fourteen young Jefferson rode from the family farm near Monticello to attend college in Williamsburg. He found challenging pursuits in mathematics, music, architecture; he read omnivorously; he spent five years studying law and prepared more than one thousand legal cases. At thirty, he married beautiful Martha Skelton; but when duty called him, he tore himself from his beloved family and joined the rebel assembly in Philadelphia.

Jefferson was thirty-three when he wrote the Declaration of Independence. Though he had never traveled more than four hundred miles beyond his birthplace, he spoke six languages and could read Homer and Virgil in the original. He could also "calculate an eclipse, survey an estate, tie an artery, plan an edifice, try a cause, break a horse, dance a minuet, play the violin."

Due to objections from South Carolina and Georgia, the passages in the Declaration which condemned slavery were cut from Jefferson's draft. "However, the Thing in its nature is so good," said Richard Henry Lee, who had made the original resolution for independence, "that no cookery can spoil

the dish for the palates of free men!" On July 4, 1776 the Declaration was adopted unanimously.

Jefferson became Governor of Virginia in 1779 and carried out important reforms in the war-torn province: he abolished feudal laws of inheritance, introduced free schools and libraries, reinforced the separation of Church and State. Succeeding his good friend Benjamin Franklin, he was appointed min-

*Jefferson's lifelong dream was to build a university where youth could pursue "the*

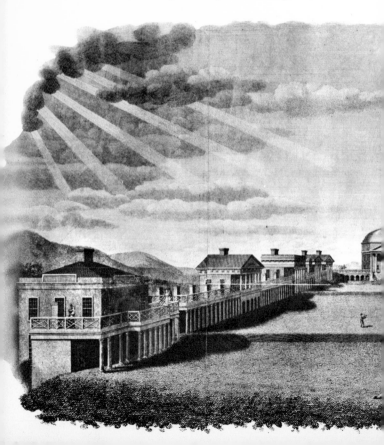

ister to France in 1785 and spent five intensely active years in Europe. Returning home, he was made Secretary of State by Washington.

The Presidential election in 1800 led to a tie between Jefferson and Aaron Burr, which was broken when Hamilton decided to cast the Federalist vote to Jefferson.

In office, he pushed through the Louisiana Purchase, buying from Napoleon

*illimitable freedom of the human mind." He founded the University of Virginia.*

for $16 million a tract which ran from the Mississippi to the Rocky Mountains —a real estate bargain at 3¢ an acre. In effect he more than doubled the size of the country without shedding a drop of blood. He launched the Lewis and Clark Expedition to explore the Northwest. He kept America from becoming embroiled in the Napoleonic Wars of Europe.

After he left the White House in 1809, he devoted his last years to founding of the University of Virginia.

An uncommon man, with abiding faith in the common people, Jefferson fought to extend the area of freedom, to give more and more men the chance to become uncommon. "There is a natural aristocracy among men," he wrote to his old friend John Adams. "The grounds of this are virtue and talent. The natural aristocracy I consider the most precious gift of nature . . ." He died at Monticello on July 4, 1826, the same day Adams died in Massachusetts.

*Summary:* JEFFERSON, THOMAS. *Born: April 13, 1743 at Shadwell, Virginia. Died: July 4, 1826 at Monticello, Virginia. Parents: Peter Jefferson and Jane Randolph. Education: William and Mary, 1762. Married: Martha Wayles Skelton, 1772; six children. Career: member of Congress, 1775-76; Governor of Virginia, 1779-81; minister to France, 1785-89; Secretary of State, 1790-93; Vice-President, 1791-1800; Third President, 1801-1809.*

# JAMES MADISON

*Father of the Constitution*

A frail, shy, studious boy, he was tutored at home in Latin, Greek, French, and Spanish. At eighteen, he left Virginia to enter the College of New Jersey where he studied Hebrew and theology with Reverend John Witherspoon, subsequently a signer of the Declaration. An ardent student of history and law, for months he slept only three hours a day.

At twenty-three, he became member of the Virginia legislature, supported Governor Jefferson's reform program, and helped draft the Virginia Plan, which had strong influence in shaping the U.S. Constitution. At thirty-six, he shared Chairman Washington's table in the State House at Philadelphia and took shorthand notes on the proceedings of the Constitutional Convention.

He was active in framing the Constitution in 1787 and in urging its adoption by the thirteen states. Though honored as Father of the Constitution, he himself was too modest to accept the honor. The Constitution was not "the off-spring of a single brain," it was "the work of many heads and many hands." More than any delegate, Madison labored to shape and sustain it.

He also fought to add to the original Constitution the Bill of Rights, which appears in the great charter in form of the first ten amendments, to assure every citizen as part of his birthright: *Freedom of speech . . . Freedom of the press*

*Landing in August 1814, 4000 British marines under Admiral Sir George Cockburn raided Washington and set fire to the White House and the Capitol.*

*. . . Freedom of religion . . . The right to petition . . . The right to peaceful assembly . . . The right to fair trial . . .* in addition to other specified rights.

A bachelor at forty-three, Madison was living in a boarding house in Philadelphia in 1794, when he met Dolly Payne Todd, an attractive widow of twenty-six. Madison wooed and won her.

Increasing friction with the British over the impressment of American seamen and the freedom of the sea led to the War of 1812. In one surprising raid on the capital, British marines landed and set fire to public buildings including the White House. Peace-loving Madison and his wife were obliged to escape into the Virginia woods. Criticized for America's lack of defense preparations, Madison regained his prestige with the report of Andrew Jackson's victory at New Orleans.

*Summary:* MADISON, JAMES. *Born: March 16, 1751 at Port Conway, Virginia. Died: June 28, 1836 at Montpelier, Virginia. Parents: James Madison and Eleanor Rose Conway. Education: College of New Jersey, 1771. Married: Dolly Payne Todd, 1794; one step-son. Career: member of Virginia legislature, 1775-80; member of Congress, 1780-97; Secretary of State, 1801-09; Fourth President, 1809-1817.*

*Dolly Madison, "a fine, portly, buxom dame," was a popular hostess.*

# JAMES MONROE

*Author of the Monroe Doctrine*

When news of the Declaration of Independence reached Williamsburg, eighteen-year-old Monroe quit the College of William and Mary to join Washington's revolutionary army. Six months later he took part in crossing the Delaware on Christmas night, 1776; he was in the thick of the surprise attack that routed the Hessians from Trenton, New Jersey. He fought in the battles that followed at Brandywine, Germantown, Monmouth.

After the Revolution he studied law, entered Virginia politics, served in Congress. President Washington appointed him as minister to France in 1794. An ardent supporter of the French Revolution, Monroe was popular in France; shortly after the Reign of Terror he managed to release from prison both Tom Paine and Mme. de Lafayette. Recalled in 1796, he published a five hundred page defense of his conduct in France, with a criticism of Washington's foreign policy.

Though he lost Washington's favor, Monroe was twice elected Governor of Virginia. President Jefferson sent him abroad in 1803 on missions to France, Spain, and England. Acting on Jefferson's advice, he negotiated with Napoleon the purchase of the Louisiana Territory. In less than a month he concluded this enormous transaction.

In Spain, however, he was unable to

reach agreement regarding Florida, then owned by Spain; and in England he negotiated a treaty which gave no redress for the seizure of American ships or the impressment of American seamen by the British. Jefferson repudiated Monroe's work and refused to ratify the treaty.

Disowned by two Presidents, impoverished, Monroe was ready to retire from public life. In 1811, Madison made him Secretary of State, then Secretary of War. In the War of 1812 Monroe proved himself vigorous and effective. He sent Jackson to defend the Southwest; he planned to raise the army to 100,000 men.

Elected President in 1816 in the "Era of Good Feeling," he was re-elected in 1820 by the remarkable electoral vote of 231 to 1. The single vote against him was cast by New Hampshire, in favor of John Quincy Adams, so only Washington might have the honor of a unanimous election.

The Monroe Doctrine, drafted with the aid of John Quincy Adams, was proclaimed by Monroe in his Presidential message of December 2, 1823. It became

*cured by the wisdom of their most enlightened citizens, and under which we have enjoyed unexampled felicity, their whole Nation is devoted. We owe it therefore to Candor, and to the amicable relations existing between the United States and those Powers, to declare that we should consider any attempt on their part to extend their system to any portion of this Hemisphere, as dangerous to our peace and safety. With the existing Colo-*

the keystone of American foreign policy for more than a century. Intended to curb the plans of the Holy Alliance, of Russia and Spain in particular, the Doctrine stated that the United States would consider it a threat to her security if any European power attempted fresh colonization or interfered with existing governments in the Western Hemisphere. It also stated that the United States had no designs on Europe and would not interfere in European affairs. In effect, the Monroe Doctrine served as America's second declaration of independence.

During his administration, Monroe secured peaceful boundaries with Canada, acquired Florida from Spain, supported anti-slavery measures which led to the Missouri Compromise. He aided the settlement of free Negroes in Africa. Monrovia, the capital of Liberia and the first free Negro republic, was named after Monroe.

Six years after he left the White House, he died in New York on July 4, 1831. A public servant for 50 years, he was the last of the "Virginia dynasty."

*Summary:* MONROE, JAMES. *Born: April 28, 1758 in Westmoreland County, Virginia. Died: July 4, 1831 in New York City. Parents: Spence Monroe and Eliza Jones. Education: College of William and Mary. Married: Elizabeth Kortright in 1786; three children. Career: officer in Continental Army, 1776-80; member of Congress, 1783-86; minister to France, 1794-96; Governor of Virginia, 1799-1802, 1810-11; minister to France, England, Spain, 1803-4; Secretary of State, 1811; Secretary of War, 1812-17; Fifth President, 1817-1825.*

# JOHN QUINCY ADAMS

*New England Independent*

As a boy of eight he witnessed the Battle of Bunker Hill from a rise of land on the family farm at Braintree. At eleven, he accompanied his father, John Adams, on a mission across the blockaded Atlantic; shipwrecked off the coast of Spain, they spent three months on the road to Paris, making their way on foot and by mule. A brilliant scholar, he was graduated from Harvard in 1788. Six years later he was appointed minister to the Netherlands by Washington.

Though unwilling to court popularity or to play the politician, in the course of fifty years in public life he held more varied and distinguished offices than any American before him. Misunderstood or maligned by most of his contemporaries, he was the last man to win the highest office without a party to back him. His election in 1824 was bitterly contested by Andrew Jackson who received more popular votes and would have been elected if Henry Clay of Kentucky hadn't decided to throw his electoral votes to Adams.

While in the White House he led a spartan life: he rose at five every day, built his own fire, read the Bible, bathed in the Potomac—before anyone in the capital was awake. He drew up a broad program to improve public education; he wanted to establish a national university, to build "the most complete observatory in the world," to further the arts and

sciences. Though most of his plans were
blocked by a hostile Congress, he did
succeed in sponsoring the Smithsonian
Institution.

Badly defeated by Jackson in 1829, he
retired to Braintree (Quincy) and devoted

himself to historical writing. Two years later his neighbors ventured to ask him if he would represent their district in Congress. The ex-President said yes and when the Plymouth Rock district elected him by an overwhelming vote, the dour

51

old man of sixty-four was much moved.

Returning to Washington in 1831, Congressman Adams began his longest and stormiest period of service. A life-long abolitionist, he objected to the gag rule which had been imposed in Congress to prohibit the discussion of anti-slavery petitions. "I hold the resolution to be a direct violation of the Constitution," declared Adams, launching his one-man fight with Congress. Year after year he stood on the floor and delivered forceful arguments; he submitted hundreds of new anti-slavery petitions.

Derided, censured, threatened with assassination, the tottering old man held his ground. Voice cracked with age he carried on the battle until, in 1845, the gag rule was revoked. Even his enemies came to respect "Old Man Eloquent." An unyielding champion of the rights of man, Adams was on the floor in February 1848 when he suffered a stroke. The eighty-year-old delegate from Plymouth Rock died two days later.

*Summary:* ADAMS, JOHN QUINCY. *Born: July 11, 1727 at Braintree, Massachusetts. Died: February 23, 1848, Washington, D.C. Parents: John Adams and Abigail Smith. Education: Harvard, 1788. Married: Louisa Johnson in 1797; four children. Career: minister to the Netherlands, 1794; minister to Prussia, 1797-1801; U.S. Senator, 1803-08; minister to Russia, 1809-11; minister to Great Britain, 1815-17; Secretary of State, 1817-24; U.S. Representative, 1831-48; Sixth President, 1825-29.*

*John Quincy Adams in his last years: a daguerreotype by Matthew Brady.*

# DEMOCRACY ON TRIAL

**CREDO:**
*To heal the wounds*

*of the Constitution
and preserve it*

*from further
violation; to*

*persuade my
countrymen,*

*so far as I may,
that it is not in*

*a splendid
government*

*surrounded by
powerful monopolies,*

*and aristocratic
establishments*

*that they will
find happiness*

*or their liberties'
protection, but*

*in a plain
system, void of*

*pomp, protecting
all and granting*

*favors to none . . .*
—ANDREW JACKSON

# ANDREW JACKSON

*Old Hickory*

Jackson's widowed mother struggled against great odds in a frontier region of South Carolina to maintain her family. She taught Andrew to read. He was nine when a copy of the Declaration of Independence reached their outpost and Andrew was chosen to read it to a group of forty illiterate frontiersmen, an honor which later became one of Jackson's proudest boasts.

Andrew's mother and two brothers died from hardships suffered during the Revolution. Alone in the world, young Jackson then worked as a saddler's apprentice. At eighteen he started to study law. One of his neighbors described him at this time as "the most roaring, rollicking, game-cocking, horse-racing, card-playing, mischievous fellow that ever lived in Salisbury." Becoming an attorney in Nashville at twenty-four, he married Rachel Robards under the impression that her first husband had obtained a divorce; he had not, until two years later, when the Jacksons were re-married. Defending Rachel's reputation, fiery-tempered Jackson fought a number of duels in the years to follow.

He was sent to Congress in 1796 as Tennessee's first representative, "a tall lank uncouth-looking personage . . with a queue tied in an eel skin." The next year he was elected U.S. Senator. From 1798 to 1804 he served as Judge of the Supreme Court of Tennessee. For

*In the Battle of New Orleans 12,000
British regulars marched against Andrew
Jackson's 6000 backwoodsmen who
picked off the marching British, row*

*after row. Within half an hour the battle was over. The enemy losses were: 700 killed, 1400 wounded. Jackson's losses were: 8 killed, 13 wounded.*

his legal services he was paid in bales of cotton or bear skins or land. During the War of 1812 he led 2500 volunteers in a campaign against the Creeks in Alabama. As major general he marched against the British in Florida and drove them from Pensacola.

He fought the celebrated Battle of New Orleans in January 1815 and decisively routed Sir Edward Pakenham's 12,000 veterans. His victory at New Orleans made forty-eight-year-old Jackson a national hero. In 1828, at the age of sixty-one, he defeated Adams (who described the new President as "a barbarian who could not write a sentence of grammar and hardly could spell his own name")

Emerging from the poorest and most turbulent elements of the western frontier, Jackson was the first authentic Democrat to enter the White House. His inauguration was witnessed by thousands of pioneer families who made the long journey to Washington to catch a glimpse of Old Hickory, symbol of the people's bloodless revolution. Daniel Webster reported how, after the inauguration, they poured into the White House, broke bowls of punch, stood on satin chairs with muddy boots while cheering their champion. "To the victor belong the spoils," was Jackson's policy. During his first term he fired two thousand old office-holders and gave the jobs to his followers.

A high-tempered boss who smoked a corn-cob pipe, kept his pistols oiled, and punctuated his remarks with "By the

*A hero of the common man, Old Hickory's journey from Nashville, Tennessee to the White House was a long triumphal procession . . . When he ended his speech at his inaugural in 1829, thou-*

sands of his admirers surrounded him
in a wild rush and Jackson's friends had
to form a ring around him to protect
him. He escaped with difficulty from
being crushed to death.

Eternal!", he dealt decisively with two major issues. One concerned the tariff of 1828, a tax on manufactured imports which South Carolina called the "Tariff of Abomination." If the federal government tried to collect the tax, South Carolina threatened to secede. Jackson declared: "Our Federal Union—it shall and must be preserved!" He sent a naval force to Charleston and ordered Gen. Winfield Scott to ready his troops to march. South Carolina backed down and the threat of secession was averted.

The second issue involved the Bank of the United States, which had become a huge monopoly. Determined to break its power, Jackson refused to re-charter the Bank, removed federal deposits of gold from it, and distributed the deposits among small new state banks throughout the country.

Re-elected in 1832, he continued his vigorous fight as the people's champion. A strong President, he set his mark on the age.

*Summary:* JACKSON, ANDREW. *Born: March 15, 1767 in New Lancaster County, South Carolina. Died: June 8, 1845 at the Hermitage near Nashville, Tennessee. Parents: Andrew Jackson and Elizabeth Hutchinson. Married: Rachel Donelson Robards in 1791; no children. Career: lawyer, farmer, soldier; U.S. Representative, 1796; U.S. Senator, 1797; Judge, Supreme Court of Tennessee, 1798-1804; Major General, War of 1812; Governor of Florida, 1818; Seventh President, 1829-37.*

# MARTIN VAN BUREN

*The Red Fox of Kinderhook*

Though he never went to college, he studied the ways of legislators who made his father's tavern at Kinderhook a stopping-place on their journeys between Albany and New York. At fourteen, "Little Van" worked in a law office in Kinderhook; at sixteen, he won his first case in the local constable's court where he had to stand on a bench in order to be seen by the jury; at eighteen, he was elected to a political convention.

He studied law in New York City, then in a state of political chaos. Van Buren polished his natural charm and shrewdness into a remarkable skill for conciliation. He welded the first Democratic political machine and became undisputed boss of the "Albany Regency." At thirty-nine, a U.S. Senator, he spearheaded Jackson's campaign in 1828 and was appointed Secretary of State.

Sent as minister to Great Britain in 1831, he was recalled a year later because the Senate refused to ratify his appointment. He was hated by his rivals but Jackson considered him "a true man with no guile" and groomed him to succeed in the White House. In 1836, Van Buren was elected President.

He was in office only two months when the Panic of 1837 swept the country, causing a severe economic depression. Unable to meet the demand for payment in gold, banks closed; farmers could not sell their crops; the unemployed rioted;

men fought for jobs which paid $4.00 a month. Though he knew it would cost him the next election, Van Buren held to his policy of not interfering with the economic life of the country; that government was best which governed least, he believed. As a remedy for the Panic, he proposed that federal deposits of gold be kept in an independent treasury, with sub-treasuries in key areas.

Re-nominated in 1840, he went down to the tune of *"Van! Van! Is a Used-Up Man!"* He broke with the Democrats in 1848 to become candidate of the Free Soil party with the slogan, "Free soil, free

*Van Buren's daughter-in-law, Angelica, served as his hostess in the White House.*

speech, free labor, and free men!" This split the Democratic vote and helped elect the Whig candidate, Zachary Taylor.

Surviving the Presidency for twenty years, Van Buren retired to Kinderhook where he died in 1862 at the age of eighty. (The expression O.K. originated with his supporters in the *Old Kinder*-hook Club.)

*Summary:* VAN BUREN, MARTIN. *Born: December 5, 1782 in Kinderhook, New York. Died July 24, 1862 at Kinderhook, New York. Married: Hannah Hoes in 1807; four children. Career: lawyer; state senator, 1812; attorney general, 1815; U.S. Senator, 1821-27; Governor of New York, 1829; Secretary of State, 1829-30; minister to Great Britain, 1831; Vice-President, 1832-36; Eighth President, 1837-41.*

# WILLIAM H. HARRISON

*For Tippecanoe and Tyler, Too!*

The future President attended Hampden-Sydney College and at eighteen, entered the University of Pennsylvania to study medicine. Four months later he quit to become a soldier. During the next fifty years he served as an Indian fighter, governor of the Northwest Territory, major general in the War of 1812, member of Congress, minister to Colombia.

Recalled from Bogota in 1829 by President Jackson, he spent the next dozen years on his farm at North Bend, Ohio. At sixty-one, he became clerk of the Hamilton County Court. From this modest post he reached the Presidency in a single step. The Whigs staged a huge circus-like campaign in 1840 for the hero of Tippecanoe, and the old Indian fighter won by a landslide.

At sixty-eight the oldest man to enter the White House, Harrison took his oath of office on a bitter, cold day, March 4, 1841, and delivered the longest inaugural speech on record. He caught cold and died of pneumonia one month later.

*Summary:* HARRISON, WILLIAM HENRY. *Born: February 9, 1773 at Berkeley, Virginia. Died: April 4, 1841 in Washington, D.C. Education: Hampden-Sydney College. Married: Anna Symmes in 1795; ten children. Career: Governor, Northwest Territory, 1800-1813; major general, 1813; U.S. Representative, 1816-19; U.S. Senator, 1825; minister to Colombia, 1828; county clerk, 1834-40; Ninth President, 1841.*

# JOHN TYLER

*His Accidency*

When President Harrison died, after one month in office, the strong men in government, Henry Clay and Daniel Webster, intended to dominate his successor. But in quiet Tyler they had caught a tiger by the tail. "His Accidency" used his veto power repeatedly to defeat their measures. Within six months his entire Cabinet, except Webster, resigned; and soon Tyler replaced Webster with John C. Calhoun as Secretary of State, which shifted power balance to the South.

A "states' rights" advocate, Tyler fought for the admission of Texas, a slave state. He signed the hotly-contested measure on March 3, 1844, his last day in office. He reappeared in the capitol sixteen years later as head of a peace committee from Virginia. Ignored, Tyler declared that Virginia would exercise her rights as a sovereign state, and secede. Elected to the Confederate Congress, Tyler died in January 1862 shortly before the rebel congress convened.

*Summary:* TYLER, JOHN. *Born: March 29, 1790 in Greenway, Charles City County, Virginia. Died: January 18, 1862 in Richmond, Virginia. Education: William and Mary, 1807. Married: Letitia Christian in 1813; seven children; and Julia Gardiner in 1844; seven children. Career: lawyer; member of Virginia legislature, 1811-16; U.S. Representative, 1816-21; Governor of Virginia, 1825-27; U.S. Senator, 1827-29, 1833-36; Vice-President, 1841; Tenth President, 1841-45.*

# JAMES KNOX POLK

*"Manifest Destiny"*

The first dark horse to win the race, Polk was the eighth Southerner to become President. He was a thin, frail, sickly boy, rather shy and secretive. At college he won top honors in mathematics and the classics. At twenty, as member of the Tennessee legislature, he secured passage of a bill against dueling. Next year he was sent to Congress. At forty-nine he was elected President.

At the start of his term he stated his four objectives: to reduce the tariff, to establish an independent treasury, to settle the Oregon boundary dispute, to secure the admission of California. He carried out his ambitious program in a single term, which was marked by the Mexican War. Three months after he left the White House in March 1849, he was dead, a victim of illness and overwork. Historian George Bancroft considered him "one of the very best, most honest and most successful Presidents the country ever had."

*Summary:* POLK, JAMES KNOX. *Born: November 2, 1795 in Mecklenburg County, North Carolina. Died: June 15, 1849 in Nashville, Tennessee. Education: University of North Carolina, 1818. Married: Sarah Childress in 1824; no children. Career: lawyer; member of Tennessee legislature, 1823-25; member of Congress, 1825-39; Speaker of the House, 1835-39; Governor of Tennessee, 1839; Eleventh President, 1845-49.*

# ZACHARY TAYLOR

*"Old Rough and Ready"*

A short dumpy man with little interest in politics, General Taylor had been a soldier for forty years. He had never cast a vote nor held a public office. When the Whigs mailed him their nomination for President in 1848, he sent the letter back unopened: there was 10¢ worth of postage due on the letter and Taylor refused to pay it.

But the Whigs were bent on putting him in the White House. They waged a campaign for him which outdid in ballyhoo the campaign they had waged for Harrison in 1840. They built up "Old Rough and Ready" as the hero of the Mexican War, the greatest soldier on the continent. At Buena Vista, General Taylor and his 5000 volunteers had defeated General Santa Anna's army of nearly 20,000 men.

President Polk, who did not have too high an opinion of Taylor, regretted his nomination. But Taylor won the election and was inaugurated in March 1849, at the age of sixty-four, becoming Chief Executive of a nation which now numbered twenty-three million people. Though he himself was a Southerner, and a slave-holder, and though four of his seven Cabinet members were Southerners, Taylor proved steadfast in his loyalty to the Union, even in the face of threats of secession. He pleaded for a cessation of sectional disputes in his message to Congress in 1849. But he was largely ignored by Congress. The Compromise of 1850 provided for the admission of California as a free state, with slavery optional in Utah and New Mexico. It abolished slave trade, but not slavery, in the District of Columbia. It included the drastic Fugitive Slave Act. President Taylor opposed the last as an appeasement of the South, but he was over-ruled. It provided for the return of runaway slaves to their owners and its cruel enforcement led to the creation of the "underground railway." Here was the inspiration for Harriet Beecher Stowe's novel "Uncle Tom's Cabin" which provided Northern sympathizers with a picture of life in the slavery-ridden South. The book became a political weapon for abolitionists and a further source of irritation for slave owners; the conflict was a prelude to civil war.

Participating in the ceremony for laying the cornerstone of the Washington Monument on July 4, 1850, Taylor stood long in the broiling sun. When he returned to the White House he drank iced milk and ate handfuls of fresh cherries. Within an hour he was ill with *cholera morbus;* and died five days later.

*Summary:* TAYLOR, ZACHARY. *Born: November 24, 1784 in Orange County, Virginia. Died: July 9, 1850 in Washington, D.C. Education: common school. Married: Margaret Smith in 1810; six children. Career: Indian fighter, army lieutenant, 1808; major, War of 1812; colonel, Black Hawk War, 1832; brigadier general, 1845; Twelfth President, 1849-50.*

# MILLARD FILLMORE

*Last of the Whigs*

For nine months out of the year he worked on his father's farm; for three months he went to a one-room school where his teacher was Abigail Powers, his future wife. Until he was nineteen and bought himself a dictionary, he had no books in his home.

At fifty, he became President. A Northern man with Southern principles, he endorsed the Compromise of 1850 and the Fugitive Slave Act. Thus he put an end to his own political future and signed the death warrant of the Whigs.

During his administration he sent Peary with a fleet to Japan and opened up trade with that empire. He received the Hungarian freedom-fighter, Lajos Kossuth, but refused to intervene in Hungary's fight against Hapsburg domination.

In his last message to Congress he opposed the accession of Cuba as a new state in the Union. He made another bid for the Presidency in 1856, becoming candidate of the Know-Nothing party, but carried only one state, Maryland.

*Summary:* FILLMORE, MILLARD. *Born: January 7, 1800 in Cayuga County, New York. Died: March 8, 1874 in Buffalo, New York. Education: common school. Married: Abigail Powers in 1826; two children; and Caroline McIntosh in 1858; no children. Career: lawyer; New York legislature, 1829-32; member of Congress, 1833-43; Comptroller of New York State, 1848; Vice-President, 1849-50; Thirteenth President, 1850-53.*

# FRANKLIN PIERCE

*The Dark Horse from New Hampshire*

Pierce was unknown to the country at large, unambitious for political honors, and did not seek the Presidency. Though a fluent orator and as handsome as a matinee idol, he made no campaign speeches; yet he defeated General Winfield Scott, the Whig candidate, by the overwhelming electoral vote of 254 to 42.

A convivial gentleman, fond of gay society, Pierce knew tragedy in his domestic life. His beautiful bride had a morbid aversion to social life; on her wishes he had resigned from the Senate and retired to Concord. His three sons all died at an early age.

As President, Pierce yielded to the pro-slavery pressure groups in Congress. He signed the Kansas-Nebraska Bill in 1854 which led to armed conflict in Kansas where a civil war in miniature took place. Defeated for re-election, Pierce returned to Concord where he died thirteen years later, discarded by his party and forgotten by his former friends.

*Summary:* PIERCE, FRANKLIN. *Born: November 23, 1804 in Hillsboro, New Hampshire. Died: October 8, 1869 in Concord, New Hampshire. Education: Bowdoin, 1824. Married: Jane Means Appleton in 1834; three children. Career: lawyer; member of New Hampshire legislature, 1829-33; U.S. Representative, 1833-37; U.S. Senator, 1837-42; brigadier general, Mexican War, 1847; Fourteenth President, 1853-57.*

# JAMES BUCHANAN

*The "Do-Nothing" President*

Son of an immigrant from Ireland, he grew up on his father's farm in Pennsylvania. Graduating from college at the head of his class he went into law. Before he was thirty he had earned $300,000 from legal fees.

A career diplomat with more experience than anyone since John Quincy Adams, he was sent as minister to Russia by President Jackson; Polk chose him for his Secretary of State; Pierce made him minister to England. The Democratic nomination came to him upon his return from England in 1856, when he felt he was too old to enjoy the honor. Backed by Northern industrial interests which feared the South's threats to secede if the Republicans came into power, Buchanan won the electoral vote. But at sixty-five, he had grown too cautious and was too indecisive to cope with the problem of secession. Facing both ways and standing still, through executive inertia he pushed the country into Civil War.

*Summary:* BUCHANAN, JAMES. *Born: April 23, 1791 in Mercersburg, Pennsylvania. Died: June 1, 1868 in Lancaster, Pennsylvania. Education: Dickinson College, 1809. Bachelor. Career: lawyer; member of Pennsylvania legislature, 1814-16; U.S. Representative, 1821-31; minister to Russia, 1832-33; U.S. Senator, 1834-45; Secretary of State, 1845-49; minister to Great Britain, 1853-56; Fifteenth President, 1857-61.*

# CIVIL WAR & RECONSTRUCTION

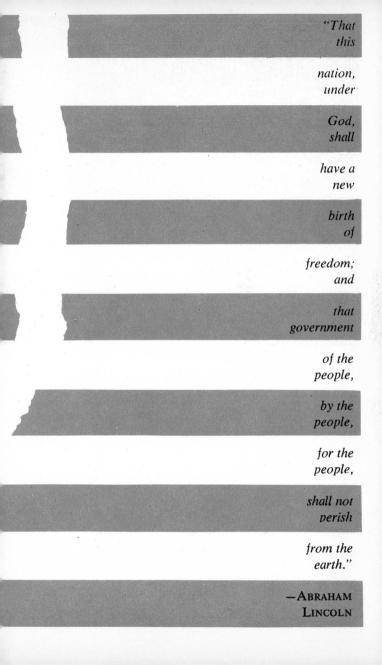

"That this

nation, under

God, shall

have a
new

birth
of

freedom;
and

that
government

of the
people,

by the
people,

for the
people,

shall not
perish

from the
earth."

—ABRAHAM
LINCOLN

# ABRAHAM LINCOLN

*The Great Emancipator*

A carpenter's son, he grew up in the Kentucky territory. His father could neither read nor write. His mother, unable to withstand the hardships of pioneer life, died on October 5, 1818 when the boy was nine. While Thomas Lincoln whipsawed a log into planks for her coffin, young Abe silently whittled wooden pegs to serve as nails for her coffin. Together they buried the wife and mother in an unmarked grave near Pigeon Creek.

A year later the father married Sarah Bush Johnston, a kindly widow with three children of her own. She brought warmth and order into the desolate cabin. Despite the father's objections, she sent young Lincoln to school whenever he could be spared from his chores. Altogether his schooling lasted less than a year. The rest he taught himself.

At sixteen, young Abe "Linkern" was known in the backwoods for his strength and his gift as a story-teller. He could sink an axe deeper into wood than anyone else. At eighteen, he stood six-feet-three and weighed nearly 200 pounds. "He looked as if he had been rough-hewn with an axe and needed smoothing with a jack-plane," said his father. The family pulled up stakes and moved farther west, to Indiana, to Illinois. Young Lincoln helped his father clear land and build a new cabin. To fence ten acres on the north side of the Sangamon, he cut down locust trees and split them into rails; one

summer, with the help of his cousin Dennis Hanks, he split three thousand rails. He floated a flatboat loaded with produce to New Orleans, where the sight of a Negro slave market made a lasting impression on him.

At twenty-one, he left his father's farm for New Salem, a village of twenty cabins and one hundred inhabitants, his home for the next five years. "A piece of floating driftwood," Lincoln called himself, "accidentally lodged at New Salem." Mill hand, store clerk, postmaster, he did whatever came his way. His native wit and kindliness won him friends. When his boss, Denton Offutt, boasted that his new clerk could "outrun, whip or throw down any man in Sangamon County," young Lincoln was challenged by the Clary Grove Boys. He fought their leader in a wrestling match and defeated the terror of the countryside.

When the Governor of Illinois called for volunteers in the Black Hawk War, twenty-three-year-old Lincoln enlisted; the Clary Grove Boys elected him their captain; they marched toward the south of Ottawa, looking for Indians. Returning within a few weeks, Lincoln ran for the Illinois legislature, and lost the county election. In New Salem he read Shakespeare and Burns, Paine and Voltaire as part of his self-education. He studied Blackstone. With the help of Mentor Graham, the village schoolmaster, he

*Lincoln credited his election to this photograph and the Cooper Union speech.*

(1) "BREAKING THE BACK OF THE REBELLION."

(2) General McClellan (Democratic nominee). "ALAS, POOR YORICK."

(3) "THE RAILSPLITTER"—a familiar caricature.

(4) Presidential aspirants, "MEASURING LINCOLN'S SHOES."

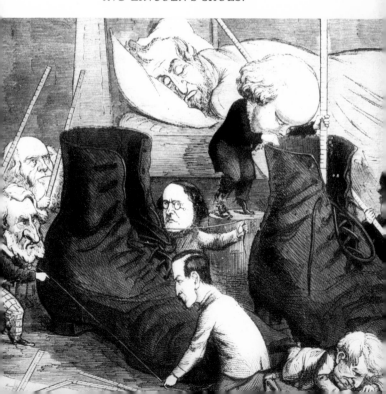

*Back from his debates with Douglas, Lincoln salutes his Springfield friends.*

studied Euclid and learned the art of surveying. In debates in Rutledge Tavern he developed as a speaker.

His deepest attachment in New Salem was Ann Rutledge, a lovely auburn-haired girl of eighteen when Lincoln first met her. She looked with sympathy at the gaunt young man of the people, they planned to get married, but the chills and fevers of malaria came to New Salem in the spring of 1835, and Ann was buried at twenty-two. For weeks Lincoln roamed the countryside like one who had lost his reason.

Packing his worldly goods in two saddlebags, he then rode to Springfield, the state capital twenty miles away, which became his home for the next thirty years.

He never returned to New Salem.

Admitted to the bar in 1837, he went into partnership in a law office with John Stuart, then with William Herndon. As a circuit lawyer he spent years on horseback riding through fourteen counties. The people of the Illinois prairies came to love and respect their homely visitor who "dripped with melancholy" yet could tell the best jokes. In 1842, Lincoln married Mary Todd, a belle from Lexington, Kentucky, who had been courted by Stephen A. Douglas. A devoted father of four sons, Lincoln endured his wife's high temper and her impatience with his slow progress. When Douglas was already a national figure, Lincoln was still an obscure country lawyer who chopped his own wood and curried his own horse.

In 1858, when the slavery issue was agitating the whole country, Lincoln engaged in a series of eight public debates with Senator Douglas. "A house divided against itself cannot stand," declared Lincoln. "This government cannot endure permanently half slave and half free." The debates brought Lincoln into national prominence. In 1860, the newly formed Republican party nominated him for the Presidency. The opposition decried Lincoln as "a nullity, a maker of clumsy jokes, a third-rate country lawyer who resembles a gorilla." Running against Senator Douglas, Lincoln got only 40% of the popular vote. But the Democrats were divided, and Lincoln won by an electoral vote of 180 to 123.

Leaving for his inauguration on a rainy morning in February 1861, he said farewell to his neighbors in Springfield. "No one, not in my position, can appreciate my feeling of sadness at this parting," said the fifty-two-year-old son of the people. "To this place and the kindness of these people I owe everything. Here I have lived a quarter of a century, and have passed from a young to an old man. Here my children have been born, and one is buried. I now leave, not knowing when or if ever I may return. Pray for me." Bareheaded in the rain, his countrymen silently watched him as the train pulled out.

Less than six weeks after his inaugural, the civil war became a grim reality. South Carolina seceded from the Union, followed by six other states. Southern troops bombarded Fort Sumter, shot down the flag, captured the fort. On April 15, 1861, Lincoln called for volunteers, and the North responded as one man.

So began the long bitter fratricidal war between the States. For four years Lincoln stood at the helm; a man of peace, he faced agonizing problems and made decisions of life and death day after day. "In times like the present," he said, "men should utter nothing for which they would not willingly be responsible through time and eternity." The struggle was marked by bloody battles at Bull Run, Shiloh, Antietam; at Fredericks-

*Lincoln, at the time of his first inaugural, in March 1861 . . . His wife, Mary Todd, a high-tempered socially ambitious belle from Lexington, Kentucky.*

96

burg, Chancellorsville, Gettysburg; at Vicksburg, Cold Harbor, Atlanta . . . Before the end of the Civil War more than two million troops were engaged and the casualties exceeded 640,000.

Lincoln issued his Emancipation Proclamation on January 1, 1863, giving political freedom to three million Negroes in the South. In November of the same year he dedicated a new cemetery at Gettysburg and spoke "half a dozen words of consecration" . . . At his second inaugural, in March 1865, he reviewed the tragic years and prepared to restore and rehabilitate the nearly van-

*General George McClellan was discharged by Lincoln early in the war.*

*When he visited the battlefields, Lincoln was accompanied by Alan Pinkerton.*

quished South. "With malice toward none, with charity for all . . . to bind up the nation's wounds, to care for him who shall have borne the battle, and for his widow and his orphan; to do all which may achieve and cherish a just and lasting peace among ourselves and with all nations."

On April 9, 1865, Lee surrendered at Appomattox. On the evening of April 14, while Lincoln was attending a play at Ford's Theater, the actor John Wilkes Booth fired a bullet into his brain. Lincoln was carried into a rooming-house across the street. Stretched on a bed too

*One of the last portrait photographs of the martyred President.*

short for his gaunt body, he died the next morning at 7:22. One among his millions of mourners, Walt Whitman said, "He leaves for America's history and biography the greatest, best, most characteristic, artistic and moral personality."

*Summary:* LINCOLN, ABRAHAM. *Born: February 12, 1809 in Hardin County, Kentucky. Died: April 15, 1865 in Washington, D.C. Parents: Thomas Lincoln and Nancy Hanks. Married: Mary Todd in 1842; four children. Career: rail-splitter, postmaster, surveyor, circuit lawyer; member, Illinois legislature, 1834-41; U.S. Representative, 1847-49; Sixteenth President, 1861-65.*

*On quiet evenings in the White House he was fond of reading to his family.*

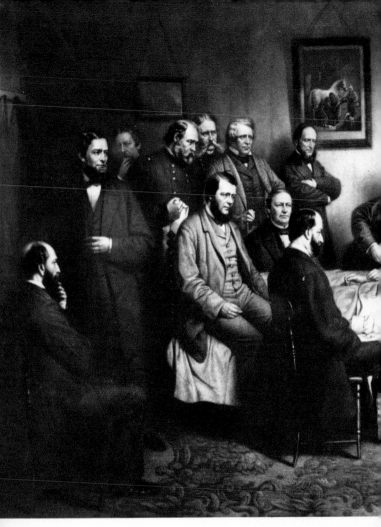

*Less than six weeks after his second in-
augural he was shot by a Southern
fanatic. Carried into a rooming house
opposite Ford's Theater, Lincoln did not
regain consciousness. Doctors, Cabinet*

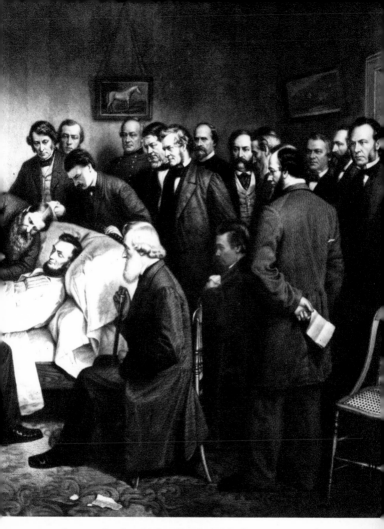

members and other high officials held all-
night vigil. Lincoln died at 7:22 A.M.
on April 15, 1865. "Now he belongs to
the ages," said Edwin M. Stanton, his
Secretary of War.

# ANDREW JOHNSON

*Father of the Homestead Act*

His conciliatory policies toward the defeated South offended Thaddeus Stevens, Edwin M. Stanton, and other vengeful "reconstructionists." Blocked by Congress, Johnson went on a speaking tour; wherever he went he was shouted down and humiliated. A bold pugnacious man, Johnson then tried to remove Stanton who refused to give up his post as Secretary of War. Stevens instigated the President's impeachment for "high crimes and misdemeanors."

The unprecedented trial opened on March 5, 1868. The majority in the Senate voted to convict the President. But the final tally, 35-19, was one vote less than the required two-thirds majority. Johnson was saved by a single vote. . . . The Tennessee Tailor was not renominated in 1868. Seven years later, elected to the Senate, he took his seat but died the same year. His tailor shop in Tennessee became a museum.

*Summary:* JOHNSON, ANDREW. *Born: December 29, 1808 in Raleigh, North Carolina. Died: July 31, 1875 at Carter's Depot, Tennessee. Parents: Jacob and Mary McDonough Johnson. Married: Eliza McCardle in 1827; five children. Career: master tailor; alderman, 1828; mayor, 1830; member of Tennessee legislature, 1835-43; U.S. Representative, 1843-53; Governor of Tennessee, 1853-57; U.S. Senator, 1857-61; military governor of Tennessee, 1862; Vice-President, 1864; Seventeenth President, 1865-69.*

*President Johnson did not attend his trial: expecting to be convicted by the Senate, he was in the White House, packing and preparing to leave.*

# ULYSSES S. GRANT

*Hero of Appomattox*

Graduating from West Point at twenty-one, he was stationed in St. Louis, Missouri. Grant wanted to resign from the army to teach mathematics, but the Mexican War intervened. Promoted to captain in 1853 he still found his pay insufficient to support his family, and resigned, returning to the Middle West.

He then tried farming in Missouri but was obliged to sell his farm at an auction. He tried selling real estate but did not prosper. At thirty-nine he was a glum, stubby, round-shouldered clerk in his father's leather shop in Galena, and the world considered him a failure.

The same year Lincoln issued the call for volunteers and Grant joined the 21st Illinois. In the next four years, the tragic years of the Civil War, Grant led the Union armies in a series of major battles and became the most celebrated general in America. On April 9, 1865, when Lee surrendered to Grant at Appomattox Court House with 27,000 men, Grant let the rebel officers keep their swords. He let the men keep their horses and mules for the spring plowing.

Grant hated the sound of drums; he hated war and politics; he never swore; he refused to listen to off-color stories. At forty-six, the Hero of Appomattox was elected President. Running against Horace Greeley, editor of the *New York Tribune,* Grant was re-elected in 1872. His second term was marked by a Wall

*DECISION AT COLD HARBOR: an early "candid camera" shot of the Civil War . . . On June 1, 1861 Grant was*

an unknown soldier; eight months later
he was a major general, having captured
Forts Henry and Donelson.

*President Grant with family and friends at Cottage-by-the-Sea in 1875, at the end of his second term which was marred by Wall Street panic.*

OFF TO THE BALL. At the Republican Convention in 1880, Grant and Blaine lost the nomination. James Garfield ("Cinderella") won on the 35th ballot.

Street panic which wiped out 23,000 small businessmen and put J. P. Morgan on top of the financial heap.

The Republican party tried to run Grant for a third term in 1876 but failed. After making a tour of the world, the former President returned home; in need of funds, he was persuaded to lend his name to a Wall Street investment firm. The firm of Grant & Ward collapsed in the Panic of 1884, with a loss of more than $16 million. Grant's partner, convicted of fraud, was sentenced to ten years imprisonment. Grant, exonerated, was left penniless.

Living on borrowed sums, Grant now started to write his *Memoirs*. A disillusioned and dying man, afflicted with cancer of the throat, he doggedly pursued the task and completed the two volumes in July 1885, four days before he died. The *Memoirs* of the Civil War hero brought $450,000 to his family, more money than Grant had earned in his lifetime. His body is buried in a great tomb on Riverside Drive in New York City.

*Summary:* GRANT, ULYSSES SIMPSON. *Born: April 27, 1822 at Point Pleasant, Ohio. Died: July 23, 1885 in New York. Parents: Jesse and Hannah Simpson Grant. Education: West Point, 1843. Married: Julia Dent in 1848; four children. Career: soldier, farmer, clerk; rose from lieutenant to General of the Army, 1843-66; Eighteenth President, 1869-77.*

*Grant at work on his celebrated* Memoirs *on June 27, 1885—twenty years after the outbreak of the Civil War and less than one month before his death.*

# RUTHERFORD B. HAYES

*A Disputed Election*

After the returns were counted, in 1876, Hayes believed that he had lost the race to the Democratic candidate, Samuel J. Tilden. But Hayes's backers refused to admit defeat. They contested 22 electoral returns from the South. Congress appointed an Electoral Commission. Behind the scenes certain electors were persuaded to change their vote. When the final tally was made, two days before the inaugural, the vote stood in Hayes's favor. The indignant Democrats called him "His Fraudulency."

Pushed into the White House, Hayes ignored his backers. He named his own Cabinet; launched Civil Service reforms; refused to inflate the currency; withdrew the last of the federal troops from the South. He sent troops to terminate the railroad strike of 1877 which had halted the nation's traffic. . . . Though his party called him a renegade, Hayes was more popular when he left the White House than when he entered it.

*Summary:* HAYES, RUTHERFORD BIRCHARD. *Born: October 4, 1822 in Delaware, Ohio. Died: January 17, 1893 in Fremont, Ohio. Parents: Rutherford and Sophia Birchard Hayes. Education: Kenyon College, 1842; Harvard Law, 1845. Married: Lucy Webb in 1852; eight children. Career: city attorney, 1858-61; major general, 1864; U.S. Representative, 1864-67; Governor of Ohio, 1867-71, 1876; Nineteenth President, 1877-81.*

119

# JAMES A. GARFIELD

*A Scholar-President*

Precocious in school, he was an avid reader of history and poetry. At twenty he entered Hiram College and earned his expenses as the school janitor. He finished his studies at Williams College, graduating with high honors in 1856. A husky blond-bearded man of twenty-five, he returned to Hiram College as professor of Greek and Latin.

Garfield distinguished himself in the Civil War and at thirty was made brigadier general, the youngest in the army. He served in the House for sixteen years. At the Republican convention in 1880 he was nominated for President on the 36th ballot. A dark horse candidate, he won the election by a narrow margin.

During his four months in the White House he was distracted constantly by hungry job-seekers. On July 2, 1881, he left to deliver a speech at Williams College; while waiting for his train in the Washington depot, he was approached by a disgruntled office-seeker, Charles Guiteau, who fired two fatal bullets into his body.

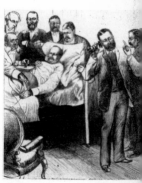

*Summary:* GARFIELD, JAMES ABRAM. *Born: November 19, 1831 at Orange, Ohio. Died: September 19, 1881 at Elberon, New Jersey. Parents: Abram and Eliza Ballou Garfield. Education: Williams College, 1856. Married: Lucretia Rudolph in 1858; seven children. Career: professor of Greek and Latin, 1856-60; major general, 1863; U.S. Representative, 1863-80; Twentieth President, 1881.*

# CHESTER A. ARTHUR

*Beau Brummel at the Helm*

At nineteen, after teaching for a year, he studied law, then established himself as a lawyer in New York City. In 1871, President Grant appointed him Collector of the Port of New York, a job which made Arthur an important dispenser of political patronage.

A protégé of the Republican boss, Senator Roscoe Conkling, Arthur became Garfield's running mate in 1880; and less than a year later, upon Garfield's assassination, Arthur was President. A handsome man of fifty-two, he was the most stylishly-dressed occupant of the White House since Van Buren. But in office he did not follow the style expected of him by his sponsors. Breaking with Conkling, he refused to indulge political spoilsmen. Instead, he appointed a Civil Service Commission and established the merit system of competitive tests for federal jobs. Dropped by his party, he died of apoplexy a year after he left the White House.

*Summary:* ARTHUR, CHESTER ALAN. *Born: October 5, 1830 in Fairfield, Vermont. Died: November 18, 1886 in New York City. Parents: Rev. William and Malvina Stone Arthur. Education: Union College, 1848. Married: Ellen Lewis Herndon in 1859; three children. Career: lawyer; Quartermaster General, 1861-65; Collector of Port of New York, 1871-80; Vice-President, 1881; Twenty-first President, 1881-85.*

# GROVER CLEVELAND

*"Grover the Good"*

The son of a poor Presbyterian clergyman, he intended to enter Hamilton College but poverty obliged him to change his plans. At sixteen, he was an assistant teacher in an asylum for the blind. At eighteen, he began studying law and was admitted to the bar in 1859. At twenty-six, he was elected Sheriff of Erie County; at forty-four, mayor of Buffalo; a year later, Governor of New York.

Honest, stubborn, independent, Cleveland was known for his ability to say no to Tammany Hall politicians. Exercising his veto repeatedly, he turned down legislative proposals with such annotations as "barefaced jobbery," "unblushing peculation," "shabby . . . inexcusable." His conduct won him the support of a Republican reform group nicknamed the Mugwumps. "We love him for the enemies he has made," said a Democratic spokesman urging his nomination for the Presidency in 1884. His election, closely contested, was inadvertently aided by Reverend Samuel Birchard; at a reception for the Republican candidate, the Reverend called the Democratic party the party of "Rum, Romanism, and Rebellion." Played up in the press, the statement alienated Catholic voters, split the Republicans, and helped swing the election to Cleveland.

A huge bull-necked bachelor of forty-eight, the new President became one of the most industrious Chief Executives.

GROVER CLEVELAND,
PRESIDENT OF THE UNITED STATES.

He fought to prevent frauds in the disposal of public lands; vetoed numerous "pork barrel" bills; advocated reduction of high tariff, which offended big business. In 1886, Cleveland married Frances Folsom, twenty-two. Before leav-

FRANCES C. FOLSOM.

*Frances Folsom was the daughter of
Cleveland's former law partner in Buffalo.*

ing the White House on March 4, 1889
—an hour before the Harrisons moved
in—Mrs. Cleveland told the staff: "Take

good care of the furniture. We are coming back just four years from today." Her prediction came true. After Harrison's term, Cleveland was again elected, in a sweeping victory, and returned to the White House on March 4, 1893 as the 24th President.

His second administration was marked by the Panic of 1893, followed by bank failures, thousands of bankruptcies, armies of jobless. During the great Pullman Strike, organized by Eugene V. Debs in 1894, Cleveland called out the troops. "If it takes the entire army and navy of the United States to deliver a post card in Chicago, that card will be delivered," said Cleveland. His conduct cost him labor's support.

In 1896 Cleveland's party nominated William Jennings Bryan for President. Bryan had been spokesman for the Populist party which voiced the farmers' grievances. Though the Democrats adopted Bryan and much of the Populist program, the Republican candidate William McKinley was elected. Grover Cleveland retired to Princeton where he died in 1908. His last words were: "I have tried so hard to do the right."

*Summary:* CLEVELAND, STEPHEN GROVER. *Born: March 18, 1837 in Caldwell, New Jersey. Died: June 24, 1908 in Princeton, New Jersey. Parents: Richard F. and Ann Neale Cleveland. Education: common school. Married: Frances Folsom in 1886; five children. Career: lawyer; Sheriff of Erie County, 1863-70; Mayor of Buffalo, 1881; Governor of New York, 1882-84; Twenty-second and Twenty-fourth President, 1885-89, 1893-97.*

*A bachelor at 49, President Cleveland married in the White House in 1886.*

*Ex-President Cleveland with wife and family at home in Princeton, New Jersey.*

# BENJAMIN HARRISON

*A Minority President*

Born on the family farm, the grandson of William Henry Harrison attended a small Ohio college, and studied law in Cincinnati. During the next twenty years he served as court reporter, city attorney, colonel in the Civil War. In 1886 he was sent to the Senate but was not re-elected. Returning home, he called himself a "dead duck" and at fifty-four considered his career finished.

But the Republican convention in 1888 picked him to run against Grover Cleveland. Big business contributed the biggest campaign fund on record. Though the popular vote went to Cleveland, Harrison won the electoral vote. The new Administration pushed through the highest protective tariff thus far enacted. It voted the treasury surplus to Northern veterans of the Civil War.

During Harrison's term six new states were admitted to the Union and Oklahoma was opened to settlers. Harrison lost the election of 1892 to Cleveland. Retiring from the political scene, he died in Indianapolis in 1901.

*Summary:* HARRISON, BENJAMIN. *Born: August 20, 1833, North Bend, Ohio. Died: March 13, 1901, Indianapolis, Indiana. Education: Miami University, 1848. Married: Caroline Scott in 1853; Mary Dimmick in 1896, three children. Career: court reporter, city attorney, 1852-60; army colonel, 1861; U.S. Senator, 1886; Twenty-third President, 1889-93.*

# WILLIAM McKINLEY

*Liberator of Cuba*

When the Civil War broke out, McKinley enlisted. In four years he rose from private to major. After the war he studied law. At thirty-four he was sent to Congress where he served in the House for the next twelve years. Elected Governor of Ohio in 1891, he did much to improve the state's roads and institutions.

Mark Hanna of Ohio backed him as the Republican candidate in 1896. Promising the return of the "full dinner pail," McKinley was elected. In office, he preserved the gold standard, raised the tariff, pursued an "Open Door" policy in China. Though opposed to intervention in Cuba, which then was in a state of rebellion against Spain, McKinley negotiated with Spain to secure the removal of the ruthless colonial governor. To protect American lives in Cuba, he sent the battleship *Maine* to Havana in February, 1898. When the ship was mysteriously blown up resentment in the United States reached the fever point. On April 11 McKinley asked Congress to declare war against Spain. In the course of the Spanish-American War, which lasted 113 days, Colonel Teddy Roosevelt led his Rough Riders in the charge on San Juan Hill, General Nelson Miles took Puerto Rico, and Commodore George Dewey steamed into Manila with six ships and took the Philippines, without losing a ship or a man. On October 10, 1898,

Spain signed a peace treaty, ceding to the United States her lost islands. Cuba was granted her independence. At the same time, Hawaii was annexed.

Re-elected in 1900, McKinley was attending the Pan-American Exposition in Buffalo when a young man stepped up as if to greet him and fired two fatal bullets.

*Summary:* **McKinley, William.** *Born: January 29, 1843 in Niles, Ohio. Died: September 14, 1901 in Buffalo, New York. Parents: William and Nancy Allison McKinley. Married: Ida Saxton in 1871; two children. Career: major in Civil War; member of Congress, 1876-1890; Governor of Ohio, 1891-94; Twenty-fifth President, 1897-1901.*

*A last picture of President McKinley taken shortly before his assassination in 1901. His assassin, anarchist Leon Czolgosz, was tried and electrocuted.*

# TWENTIETH CENTURY LEADERS

The American purpose
remains what it

has been since the
nation's founding:

to demonstrate
that the organization

of men and
societies on the

basis of human
freedom is not

an absurdity,
but an enriching,

ennobling, practical
achievement . . . Our

purpose is not only
to defend the

integrity of this
democratic society

but also to help
advance the cause of

human freedom
and world law—

the universal
cause of a just

and lasting peace.
—JOHN F. KENNEDY

# THEODORE ROOSEVELT

*The Rough Rider*

A puny child, afflicted with asthma and myopia, he was born in New York City in the narrow three-story brick residence at 28 East 20th Street. A seventh-generation New Yorker, he came of Dutch, French Huguenot, Scotch-Irish ancestry. His father, a glass manufacturer and banker, was a prominent civic leader.

One of Theodore's first challenges was to build up his own physique. Having been a sickly boy, with no natural prowess, he recorded in his *Autobiography*, "I was at first quite unable to hold my own. I was nervous and timid. Yet from reading of the people I admired, I felt a great admiration for men who were fearless and who could hold their own in the world, and I had a great desire to be like them." He exercised at home with Indian clubs and iron bars till he transformed his body.

At sixteen, he entered Harvard. "My ambition was to become a scientist." He studied the natural sciences, became editor of the *Advocate* and a member of Phi Beta Kappa. Though his defective eyes limited his work with the microscope, he remained an enthusiastic amateur naturalist all his life. Graduating from Harvard in 1880, he attended Columbia Law School. At twenty-three he married Alice Hathaway Lee of Boston. Four years later his lovely young wife and his mother both died the same day, February 14, 1884. In an effort to re-

139

cover from the tragic blow, Roosevelt left New York and went into ranching in the Bad Lands of Dakota.

Working with cowboys month after month in the land of the long-horned cattle, he made friends with hundreds of westerners. From the spirit of the frontier, he drew fresh confidence in life. Returning to New York in 1886, he ran for mayor at twenty-eight and was defeated. Ten years later he was president of the New York City Police Commission. Ignoring the threats of political bosses, he fired crooked policemen, rounded up gangsters, and cleaned up the city. Within a year "Teddy the Scorcher" had become a favorite of cartoonists, and a hero of New York.

When McKinley appointed him Assistant Secretary of the Navy in 1897, he fought for a stronger navy. When war with Spain threatened, he cried: "Build a battleship in every creek!" When McKinley was reluctant to intervene in Cuba, Roosevelt said, "McKinley has no more backbone than a chocolate eclair!" Resigning his office, he led his Rough Riders in the celebrated charge up San Juan Hill and became a national hero.

Elected Governor of New York in 1898, he continued his strenuous fight against corruption and injustice. Hoping to get rid of the knight on the white horse, party bosses backed him in 1900 as the Republican candidate for the Vice-Presidency. They considered the office a

*Colonel Roosevelt and his Rough Riders who took San Juan Hill in Cuba in 1898.*

political graveyard. But McKinley's assassination suddenly changed the picture and caused Mark Hanna to exclaim, "That damned cowboy *is* in the White

*His exploit in the Spanish-American War made Roosevelt a national hero.*

House!" At 42, Theodore Roosevelt became the nation's youngest President.

As Chief Executive he vigorously pursued his Square Deal reform program.

He hunted for "malefactors of great wealth," prosecuted monopolies, broke up giant trusts in oil, sugar, meat-packing, tobacco, railroads. He launched the Department of Labor. He pushed through the Workmen's Compensation Act. He sponsored the Reclamation Act, which called for building great dams to irrigate the arid West. As part of his conservation program he fought for the preservation of forests and scenic areas, game and wildlife refuges; for the construction of fifty-one national bird sanctuaries.

As President in 1904 when German imperialists penetrated Brazil, then blockaded Venezuela, he sent a warning to Kaiser Wilhelm. When the warning was ignored, he assembled the fleet under Admiral Dewey and sent the Kaiser an ultimatum: "Withdraw from Venezuela or we open fire." The Kaiser withdrew. Roosevelt then sent the fleet on a goodwill tour around the world. "Walk softly, but carry a big stick; and you will go far," was his favorite African proverb. . . . Asked to mediate in the war between Russia and Japan in 1905, he met with delegates from both countries in New Hampshire and negotiated an acceptable peace treaty. He was the first statesman to use The Hague Court for arbitrating international disputes. Honored for his contributions to world peace, he was the first American to win a Nobel Prize.

He played a major part in building the Panama Canal. Determined to make the

dirt fly, he promoted political changes, quickly recognized the new-born Republic of Panama, put Colonel George Goethals in charge of the construction and revitalized the gigantic project. Amid his many varied pursuits he found time to read prodigiously. As avid a reader as Jefferson, he devoured entire libraries. He wrote thirty books, among which *The Winning of the West* is perhaps best known. He also wrote 150,000 letters.

Within two weeks after leaving the White House, he embarked on an expedition into Africa. "My last chance to be a boy," confessed the fifty-year-old former President. He shot lions and collected valuable specimens which he sent to the Smithsonian Institution. He toured Egypt, Europe, England. Later he traced the source of the River of Doubt in Brazil, now named Rio Roosevelt.

Back in America in 1912, displeased with William Howard Taft whom he had groomed as his successor, Roosevelt broke with the Republicans and organized the Progressive party with himself as Presidential candidate. At the polls Roosevelt received a higher popular vote than Taft; but the split in the Republican party led to the election of Woodrow Wilson, a Democrat. In 1917, when America entered World War I, Roosevelt volunteered to raise and lead a division. But President Wilson turned down the ailing warrior. In January, 1919, Roosevelt lay on his deathbed at Oyster Bay, Long Island. "Both life and

*Roosevelt with his four sons. The youngest, Quentin, died in World War I in July, 1918: he was a fighter pilot.*

death are parts of the same great adventure," observed the sixty-one-year-old Rough Rider. He was buried beside a bird sanctuary he had built.

*Summary:* ROOSEVELT, THEODORE. *Born: October 27, 1858 in New York City. Died: January 6, 1919 in Long Island, New York. Education: Harvard, 1880. Married: Alice Hathaway Lee in 1880, one child; and Edith Kermit Carow in 1887, five children. Career: rancher, explorer, writer; member, New York Legislature, 1882-84; New York City Police Commissioner, 1896-97; Assistant Secretary of Navy, 1897-98; colonel, Spanish-American War, 1898; Governor of New York, 1898-1900; Vice-President, 1900-01; Twenty-sixth President, 1901-09.*

# WM. HOWARD TAFT

*Chief Executive and Chief Justice*

His father had served as Secretary of War in Grant's cabinet and later as minister to Russia. Young William was a smiling roly-poly boy whom his schoolmates soon nicknamed "Fatty." In a play at Woodward High School in Cincinnati he played the part of Sleeping Beauty and convulsed his audience. At Yale he played baseball and football; graduating in 1878, he stood second highest in his class. He studied law, then became a court reporter in Cincinnati. A good-humored young giant, at twenty-three he waged a crusade against corruption in the Ohio law courts and helped to bring about lasting reforms. By the time he reached thirty-five he had risen from assistant district attorney to federal circuit judge. In 1898, when Spain ceded the Philippines, McKinley chose Taft to govern the distant Pacific islands.

As governor of the Philippines, Taft set up courts of justice, free · public schools, hospitals, a postal savings bank. He trained the most able natives in the principles of democratic government so they might carry on independently the work he had begun. Devoted to the Filipinos, he called them "my little brown brothers." In 1904, President Roosevelt chose Taft as his Secretary of War. Taft went on missions to Cuba, to Japan, to Panama. In each place he exercised his great skill as a conciliator. Roosevelt groomed him as his successor and helped

secure his election in 1908.

A bland mountain of a man, President Taft stood six-feet-two and weighed more than three hundred pounds; physically he was the biggest man to fill the Presidential boots. In general he carried on Roosevelt's Square Deal policies. Toward the end of his term, however, unable to deal firmly with factions in Congress, he alienated the progressives and antagonized Roosevelt, who formed the "Bull Moose" party to block Taft's re-election. When he left the White House in 1913, Taft called it "the lonesomest place in the world." From 1913 to 1921 he taught law at Yale; in 1921 Harding appointed him Chief Justice of the Supreme Court.

At sixty-four, Taft realized his greatest ambition and enjoyed the highest honor ever accorded a former President. He presided over the Supreme Court for nine years. "I don't remember that I was ever President," he remarked toward the end of his life. In February 1930 he resigned on account of illness; a month later he was buried in Arlington National Cemetery.

*Summary:* TAFT, WILLIAM HOWARD. *Born: September 15, 1857 in Cincinnati, Ohio. Died: March 8, 1930 in Washington, D.C. Parents: Alphonso and Louisa Torrey Taft. Education: Yale, 1878. Married: Helen Herron in 1886; three children. Career: lawyer; court reporter; assistant district attorney, 1881-83; judge, Ohio Superior Court, 1887; U.S. Solicitor-General, 1890; federal circuit judge, 1900; Governor of the Philippines, 1901-04; Secretary of War, 1904; Chief Justice of U.S. Supreme Court, 1921-30; Twenty-seventh President, 1909-13.*

# WOODROW WILSON

*Founder of the League of Nations*

He was a schoolmaster by vocation, a scholar by inclination, a moralist by temperament. Until he was fifty, he taught history in school. Then he became a maker of history.

Leaving Princeton University, in 1910, he ran on a reform ticket and was elected Governor of New Jersey. The record he made won him national notice. In 1912, at the Democratic convention in Baltimore, he was nominated President, on the 46th ballot. Winning the election, he left New Jersey to take his place at the "most perilous helm in Christendom."

An enemy of special privilege, he launched his "New Freedom" program and carried out a number of reforms. Advocating his measures, he would frequently appear and speak before Congress, a practice which had been abandoned since the days of John Adams. "Liberty does not consist in mere general declarations of the rights of man," he said. "It consists in the translation of those declarations into definite action." Wilson reduced the tariff, set up the Federal Trade Commission, established the Federal Reserve System; he endorsed the Farm Loan Act, the Child Labor Act, the Pure Food Act.

In 1916 he was re-elected on his pledge to keep America out of the war which then was raging in Europe. But America, after suffering unrestricted submarine attacks from Germany, could not

maintain her "splendid isolation." Wilson
went through a period of agonizing trial.
On April 2, 1917 he met with Congress
in an extraordinary session. Wilson called
Germany's recent course of action to be
nothing less than undeclared war against
the United States. "It is a fearful thing
to lead this great peaceful people into
war. But the right is more precious than
peace . . . The world must be made
safe for democracy." Four days later
Congress declared war against Germany.

Wilson spearheaded the Great Crusade: the whole country was mobilized;
shipyards and factories worked around
the clock. The nation went on an aus-
terity schedule in order to send food

*Governor Wilson of New Jersey, being
congratulated on his nomination.*

and supplies overseas. Time was of the essence, for Germany was on the verge of conquering Europe. "Our backs are to the wall," the Allies appealed to Wilson. "It is a race between Hindenburg and Wilson," declared Lloyd George. In June 1917 General John Pershing sailed for Europe: by spring next year ten thousand American marines had landed on the coast of Normandy. They fell at Belleau Woods, at Château Thierry, at Saint Mihiel, and in the Argonne Forest, but their sacrifice turned the tide of battle and forced a seemingly invincible enemy to retreat, and then to capitulate. On November 11, 1918 the Armistice was signed.

*THE BIG FOUR: Orlando, Clemenceau, Lloyd George, and Woodrow Wilson.*

*After the signing of the treaty of peace
at Versailles on June 28, 1919 . . . The
treaty was made by representatives of
Germany and the Allied powers.*

Nearly a year before the war ended,
Wilson had published his 14-Point Program which included his plan for a
League of Nations embodying his hope
of freeing mankind forever from the old
scourge of war.

When he went to Europe in December 1918, he was hailed by the long-
suffering masses as a New World mes-

siah. But the diplomats of Versailles, more concerned with punishing the aggressor than with removing the causes of war, cut much of Wilson's program. He held firmly to his idea of a League of Nations, however, and brought them to accept it, then returned home. The majority in Congress were in favor of the League. Certain Senators, however, insisted on changes in the plan: they did not want the United States to become subject to the vetoes of other nations. Wilson refused to compromise. His all-

*On board the SS* George Washington, *returning from Europe in 1919, President Wilson is confident that he has won support for the League of Nations and that Congress would ratify his measures.*

or-nothing attitude united the isolationists against him. To gain support, Wilson then went on a tour, addressing thousands in small towns throughout the Middle West and Far West. He fervently pleaded with them to remember their dead sons and fathers and to safeguard the unborn. While speaking in Pueblo, Colorado, he suffered a paralytic stroke which crippled him for the rest of his life.

On November 19, 1919, the Senate voted to enter the League, by 49 votes to 35; but the vote did not represent a two-thirds majority. The measure was defeated by seven "irreconcilables." Though most of Europe, Asia, South America joined the League, the United States never did. "A little group of willful men, representing no opinion but their own, have rendered the great government of the United States helpless and contemptible," commented Wilson.

Awarded the Nobel Peace Prize in 1919, he died in 1924, a casualty of the war to end war. "Ideas live; men die," he said. His idea lives on in the United Nations.

*Summary:* WILSON, WOODROW. *Born: December 28, 1856 in Staunton, Virginia. Died: February 3, 1924 in Washington, D.C. Parents: Rev. Joseph R. and Janet Woodrow Wilson. Education: Princeton, 1879; Ph. D., Johns Hopkins, 1886. Married: Ellen Louise Axson in 1885; three children; and Edith Bolling Galt in 1915. Career: professor of history at Bryn Mawr, Wesleyan, Princeton; president of Princeton, 1902-10; author; Governor of New Jersey, 1910-12; Twenty-eighth President, 1913-21.*

# WARREN G. HARDING

*A Dark Horse from Ohio*

At nineteen, he became a reporter on the Marion *Star*. Later, as editor and publisher, he developed it into a popular Republican party organ.

At thirty-five, he entered state politics and became known as a poker player, a vote-getter, a sonorous orator and everybody's friend. At forty-nine, he was elected to the U.S. Senate. In 1920, at the Republican convention in Chicago, his old friend Harry M. Daugherty pushed Senator Harding to the front.

Harding promised a "return to normalcy." The country at large, weary of Woodrow Wilson's austere leadership, swept him into office by a landslide. In the post-war boom era the government was active in the disposal of rich oil lands and surplus property. Scandals broke in 1923 when three members of Harding's Cabinet were charged with graft and bribery. Distressed, Harding went on a speaking tour in an effort to vindicate himself. Returning from Alaska, he fell ill and died suddenly in a San Francisco hotel on August 2, 1923.

*Summary:* HARDING, WARREN GAMALIEL. *Born: November 2, 1865 in Corsica, Ohio. Died: August 2, 1923 in San Francisco, California. Married: Florence Kling DeWolfe in 1891; one step-son. Career: editor; publisher; member, Ohio legislature, 1900-10; U.S. Senator, 1914-20; Twenty-ninth President, 1921-23.*

# CALVIN COOLIDGE

*Silent Cal*

Born on the Fourth of July in Plymouth Notch, a tiny village in Vermont, he grew up in a thrifty and taciturn community. Though slight in stature, he spent his summers working in sawmills or at logging. As a student at Amherst he won first prize for his essay on causes of the American Revolution. Graduating with high honors in 1895, he went into law practice in Northampton, Massachusetts: in the next twenty years he held nineteen elective offices, from town councilman to state governor. Frugal with words and parsimonious with the public purse, he let his record speak for itself.

When Boston's policemen went on a strike in 1919, Governor Coolidge sent out the militia and put the city under martial law. He sent a wire to the union leader Samuel Gompers: "There is no right to strike against the public safety by anybody, anywhere, anytime." His decisive action won him national notice and led to his election as Vice-President in 1920. Upon Harding's death in 1923, he became the sixth Vice-President to reach the highest office through the death of his chief.

President Coolidge quietly cleaned up the scandals of the Harding administration. Elected in his own right in 1924, he continued his cautious housekeeping while the post-war boom rose to new heights. "The business of America is

business," said Coolidge. He reduced the
national debt by two billion. A laconic
Yankee with a dry sense of humor, he
told inquiring reporters in 1927: "I do
not choose to run for President in 1928."
Bowing out to Herbert Hoover, he left
the White House and retired to Northampton. For a year he wrote a daily column of two hundred words, for which
a newspaper syndicate paid him an annual salary of $200,000. He died at
sixty-one and was buried at Plymouth

Notch. "He didn't do much," Harry S. Truman appraised his career. "Maybe there wasn't much for him to do."

*Summary:* COOLIDGE, CALVIN. *Born: July 4, 1872 in Plymouth Notch, Vermont. Died: January 5, 1933 in Northampton, Massachusetts. Parents: John Calvin and Victoria Moor Coolidge. Education: Amherst, 1895. Married: Grace Anna Goodhue in 1905; two children. Career: lawyer; rose from councilman to governor of Massachusetts, 1900-1920; Vice-President, 1921-23; Thirtieth President, 1923-29.*

# HERBERT C. HOOVER

*The Quaker Engineer*

The short husky son of a Quaker blacksmith, he was born and reared on a farm at West Branch, Iowa. At seventeen, he entered Stanford where he majored in geology and mining engineering. Earning most of his own tuition and living expenses, he graduated in 1891. He was then employed by an engineering firm in San Francisco and was entrusted to set up and operate gold mines first in Australia, then in China. At thirty, he had offices of his own throughout the world. At forty, he was a multimillionaire financier and promoter of mining properties.

During World War I, he directed a vast rehabilitation program for war-stricken Europe. Serving without pay, he gave part of his own fortune to help the victims of war. In 1921, he became Secretary of Commerce in Harding's Cabinet.

He was elected President in 1928 at the age of fifty-four. On October 29, 1929 came the stock market crash which ushered in the worst depression in modern history. Throughout America the wheels of industry stopped turning. The number of unemployed rose to seventeen millions. Hoover did not believe in federal welfare or social security programs for Americans; he felt that such aid should be rendered by private charity and kept on a local level. By the end of his term 5000 banks had closed

their doors. Farm prices were the low-
est on record. Business failures exceeded 30,000 a year. The gross national
income dropped from 80 billion to 40
billion.

"Prosperity is just around the corner,"
promised Hoover. In an effort to cope
with the breakdown he set up the Reconstruction Finance Corporation to loan
federal funds to railways, banks, states,
and municipalities. What he did was too
little and came too late. When a bonus
army of 7000 veterans marched and
camped in Washington in July 1932,
Hoover ordered their shacks burnt and
the petitioners dispersed by force. Running for re-election the same year, he

*Hoover greets Thomas Edison who first
visited the White House in 1878.*

warned the country that if the Democrats got in, "the grass will grow in the streets of a hundred cities." He received fewer electoral votes than any President campaigning for re-election since the founding of the Republic.

Hoover retired from the political arena at fifty-eight and donated a research library to Stanford University.

*Summary:* HOOVER, HERBERT. *Born: August 10, 1874 in West Branch, Iowa. Parents: Jesse Clark and Hilda Hoover. Education: Stanford, 1891. Married: Lou Henry in 1899; two children. Career: mining engineer; financier; war relief administrator, 1914-19; Secretary of Commerce, 1921-28; Thirty-first President, 1929-33.*

*Hoover and British Prime Minister Ramsay MacDonald.*

# FRANKLIN D. ROOSEVELT

*Champion of the Four Freedoms*

An only child, born on the family estate at Hyde Park, New York, he was tutored at home by his mother, Sara Delano Roosevelt, until he entered Groton. At ten he was taken on a visit to President Cleveland who patted him on the head and told him with a sigh: "My little man, I am going to make a strange wish for you. May you never be President of the United States." At Harvard Roosevelt became editor of the *Crimson,* member of the Phi Beta Kappa, and chairman of his class.

Graduating from Harvard in 1904, he attended Columbia Law School. At twenty-three, he married Eleanor Roosevelt, a fifth cousin, and an orphaned niece of President Theodore Roosevelt. At the wedding in New York in 1905 the President gave away the bride. A shy poetic personality, already devoted to the quest for social justice, Eleanor shared her husband's remarkable career: in the next four decades she took part in more far-reaching reforms than any other woman in American history.

In 1912, while serving as state senator, Roosevelt worked to secure the nomination and election of Woodrow Wilson. Next year Wilson appointed him Assistant Secretary of the Navy. At thirty the youngest man to hold the office, Roosevelt labored to build up the Navy; next to Wilson, he was the most active man in government. During World War I,

cutting through red tape to expedite preparations, he broke enough laws to send him to jail for 999 years, he remarked later. Attending the Peace Conference at Versailles in 1919, he witnessed Wilson's efforts to launch the League of Nations. Wilson and Jefferson had perhaps the strongest influence on Roosevelt's political philosophy.

In 1920 Roosevelt became Democratic candidate for Vice-President. But the country voted the Harding-Coolidge

*Franklin and Eleanor Roosevelt on their honeymoon at Campobello Island.*

ticket and Roosevelt returned to New York intending to resume his law practice. Next summer, while vacationing with his family at Campobello Island in New Brunswick, he was stricken with polio and paralyzed from the waist down. At forty he was a permanent invalid doomed to an early death. But high-spirited Roosevelt fought the faceless enemy. For three years he exercised his afflicted body. He set up a non-profit clinic in Warm Springs, Georgia to help

*The youngest Assistant Secretary of the Navy practices target shooting.*

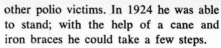

other polio victims. In 1924 he was able to stand; with the help of a cane and iron braces he could take a few steps.

At the Democratic convention in 1928 he made the nominating speech for Al Smith, "The Happy Warrior." The same year Roosevelt was elected Governor of New York. His record as governor won his re-election in 1930 and brought him national prominence. In 1932, when the country was grappling with the worst depression in its history, Roosevelt became the Democratic candidate against Herbert Hoover, and was elected by a landslide. "First of all, let me assert my firm belief," he stated in his inaugural on March 4, 1933, "that the only thing we have to fear is fear itself."

Given the broadest emergency powers ever accorded a President in time of peace, Roosevelt plunged into action to revitalize the economy and restore the promise of democracy. During his first term he set up huge public works to start the wheels of industry rolling again. He found work for the jobless, food for the hungry, shelter for the homeless. Working with his advisers, "The Brain Trust," he established scores of federal agencies: the Civilian Conservation Corps, employing three million youths, to conserve our natural resources. The Works Progress Administration, employing ten million men, to build roads and bridges, schools, hospitals, and other public buildings in hundreds of towns

*Nominated for a third term, FDR speaks in New York City in 1940.*

throughout the country. Four hundred federal projects for artists, writers, musicians, actors, to add to the nation's cultural resources. The Farm Security Administration, to help millions of farmers. Agencies to regulate the stock market, to stabilize the banks, to lend billions to hard-pressed businessmen. The Tennessee Valley Authority, to build a chain of dams to bring cheap water, power, and light to the moribund South; in addition, other giant dams in the West.

In 1936 Roosevelt was re-elected by the unprecedented electoral vote of 523 to 8 for Landon. "President Roosevelt is the only dictator by popular demand in the history of the world,"

*FDR reviews Fleet—with his mother, his wife, his daughter, and his son James.*

Will Rogers wrote in his column. During his second term Roosevelt met with increasing hostility from big business interests. They accused him of giving labor too much power and denounced "That man in the White House" as a traitor to his class. In 1940 he was re-elected.

Europe ablaze with Hitler's wars of aggression, Roosevelt tried to alert the country. He was denounced as a warmonger by the isolationists. In March 1941, Congress passed the Lend-Lease Bill empowering Roosevelt to send military supplies to Great Britain, Russia, and other countries which were trying to resist the Nazi Juggernaut. On December 7, 1941, "a day that will

*FDR and Falla—a favorite companion, known and loved by the nation.*

live in infamy," Pearl Harbor was at-
tacked by Japan—Hitler's Asiatic partner—in a raid which destroyed a large
part of the U.S. Fleet. The whole
country now stood behind Roosevelt
as he mobilized America's vast resources and declared war against the
Axis. In alliance with British and Rus-
sian leaders, the President, who was
locked in a wheel-chair, conducted war
on a global scale. After a mid-Atlantic
meeting with Winston Churchill, which
resulted in the Atlantic Charter, Roosevelt made plans to organize the United
Nations, re-affirming his goal of the
Four Freedoms:

"The first is freedom of speech and

*FDR with Churchill in 1941 meeting
which resulted in the Atlantic Charter.*

expression—everywhere in the world. The second is freedom of every person to worship God in his own way—everywhere in the world. The third is freedom from want—everywhere in the world. The fourth is freedom from fear —anywhere in the world."

Elected for a fourth term in 1944, he held a last meeting at Yalta with Stalin and Churchill, believing that the great powers could establish conditions for a durable peace. On April 12, 1945, exhausted by his labors in guiding the country through the worst depression and most destructive war in history, he died at Warm Springs, Georgia.

The world was stunned by his death.

*FDR in Sicily on December 8, 1943, with General Dwight D. Eisenhower.*

Winston Churchill called him, "The greatest champion of freedom who ever brought help and comfort from the New World to the Old."

*Summary:* ROOSEVELT, FRANKLIN DELANO. *Born: January 30, 1882 at Hyde Park, New York. Died: April 12, 1945 at Warm*

*THE YALTA CONFERENCE. A historic meeting held in 1945 by Churchill,*

Springs, Georgia. Parents: James and Sara Delano Roosevelt. Education: Harvard, 1904; Columbia Law School, 1907. Married: Anna Eleanor Roosevelt in 1905; six children. Career: lawyer; member, New York Legislature, 1910-13; Assistant Secretary of the Navy, 1913-20; Governor of New York, 1928-32; Thirty-second President, 1933-45.

Roosevelt, and Stalin to enlist Soviet aid in the struggle against Japan.

# HARRY S. TRUMAN

*"Mr. Citizen"*

Son of a horse and mule trader, he was born on the family farm in Missouri. While attending high school in Independence, he worked in the local drug store. At seventeen, he applied to West Point but was turned down on account of his eyes; he had worn thick-lensed glasses since the age of nine. Before twenty-one, he held temporary jobs as timekeeper on a railroad gang and as bookkeeper in a Kansas City bank. From the age of twenty-two to thirty-three he worked as a dirt farmer.

A member of the National Guard in 1917, he attended field artillery school in Oklahoma. Sent overseas in 1918, he saw action at St. Mihiel and Meuse-Argonne. "He was one of the fastest calculators of artillery data in the whole division," reported one of his men. Six months later, Captain Harry Truman was discharged. Back home, he opened a men's clothing store in partnership with one of his former sergeants. When the business went bankrupt in 1922, Truman took it upon himself to pay off his creditors.

He entered local politics the same year and was elected county judge. In 1934 he was elected U.S. Senator. In 1940, as chairman of a "watchdog" committee on defense expenditures, he won a national reputation for his efficiency in safeguarding the public interest. In 1945, three months after Roosevelt's inaugural, Vice-

President Truman became President.

"Last night the whole weight of the moon and the stars fell on me," he told reporters on April 13, 1945.

*THE POTSDAM CONFERENCE held August 10, 1945 at Potsdam, Germany.*

*Seated: Prime Minister Clement Attlee, President Truman, Soviet Premier Stalin. Standing: Admiral Leahy, Ernest Bevin,*

Chance and the democratic process had catapulted him into an office of awesome power. On August 6, 1945, on Truman's orders, an army plane flew

*James Byrnes, V. Molotov.*

*Through agreements reached at the Potsdam Conference the transfer of a part of East Germany to the Union of Soviet Socialist Republics was approved.*

189

over Hiroshima and dropped the atom
bomb which killed 78,000 people; on
August 9 the second bomb was dropped
over Nagasaki, killing 74,000. "It was
my responsibility as President to force
the Japanese warlords to come to terms
as quickly as possible with the minimum
loss of lives," wrote Truman. "I then
made my final decision. Almost immedi-
ately after the dropping of the second
bomb the Japanese surrendered."

The year 1945 marked the end of

*HE WHO LAUGHS LAST. The press
and radio and much of his own party
predicted Truman's defeat in 1948. But
the man from Missouri traveled some
30,000 miles in a "whistle-stop" campaign to bring to the people his case
against a "Do-Nothing" Congress which
had obstructed both his domestic and
foreign aid program. In the biggest election upset on record Truman was returned to the White House.*

World War II, the collapse of colonial empires, the birth of the United Nations. It ushered in huge problems in global reconstruction. Truman sought to provide economic and technical aid to countries throughout the world, to implement the Marshall Plan, the Truman Doctrine, the Point Four Program with billions of dollars in foreign aid. Running for election in 1948, he conducted a strenuous "whistle-stop" campaign, traveling some 30,000 miles in a "Give 'em Hell" campaign against the "Do-Nothing" Eightieth Congress. In the biggest election upset on record, he was returned to the White House. In 1949, he signed the treaty of alliance with NATO, a group of twelve Western nations pledged to mutual defense. In 1950, he sent General Douglas MacArthur to Korea, in command of United Nations forces, to stop the spread of communism in divided Korea. When MacArthur wanted to carry the conflict into Communist China, Truman relieved him of command.

Retiring to Independence, Missouri, in 1952, he devoted himself to writing his memoirs and to establishing the Truman Library. When asked what he would like for his epitaph, Truman answered: "He was a good public servant."

*Summary:* TRUMAN, HARRY S. *Born: May 8, 1884 in Lamar, Missouri. Parents: John Anderson and Martha Young Truman. Education: high school. Married: Bess Wallace in 1919; one child. Career: farmer; haberdasher; army captain, 1918; county judge, 1922-34; U.S. Senator, 1934-44; Vice-President, 1945; Thirty-third President, 1945-53.*

# DWIGHT D. EISENHOWER

*"General Ike"*

As a high school student in Abilene, Kansas, he was best in football and baseball although a class prophet predicted that, "Ike will wind up as professor of history." To earn money to go to college he worked in a dairy, eighty-four hours a week. At West Point he played football against the All-American athlete, Jim Thorpe. Graduating in 1915, he served in the army and slowly advanced in rank in the next three decades. In 1941, at the age of fifty-one, he was a colonel. On General Douglas MacArthur's staff in the Philippines, he was recognized as an outstanding strategist. In 1942, General George C. Marshall brought him into the General Staff, then put him in command of the allied invasion of North Africa. Two years later "General Ike" was made Supreme Allied Commander. On D-Day, June 6, 1944, he launched the full-scale invasion of Nazi-occupied Europe from a beachhead at Normandy, and led the most stupendous campaign in military history. On May 7, 1945 Germany surrendered unconditionally.

Hero of the crusade in Europe, Eisenhower returned home in 1945, more popular than any American soldier since General Grant. On his tour of the country, millions lined the streets and shouted themselves hoarse with, "Ike, Ike, Ike!" Removing his uniform he became president of Columbia University in 1948.

193

Though both Democrats and Republicans sought him as their candidate, he turned down each party. He told one reporter, "In the strongest language you can command you may say that I have no political ambitions at all. . . ."

In 1952, Eisenhower was drafted by the Republican party and elected by the largest popular vote in American history. In office, he followed the middle-of-the-road course. He favored foreign aid and disarmament, with guarantees. When the United States still held the monopoly on nuclear fission, he proposed his "Atoms for Peace" program, to help develop the peaceful uses of atomic energy on a worldwide basis. In 1953, he put an end to the war in Korea by negotiating a cease-fire. In 1954, he supported the Nationalist Chinese government in Formosa and the integration of West Germany with Western Europe. In 1955, he suf-

*(1) CRUSADER IN EUROPE.*

*(2) "BEST OF LUCK, IKE!"*

194

fered a heart attack which alarmed the nation. In 1956, he was re-elected, receiving a plurality of ten million popular votes over the Democratic candidate, Adlai E. Stevenson. His re-election was a personal triumph for Ike. The Republican party itself received a scant majority in Congress.

In 1957, President Eisenhower sent federal troops into Little Rock, Arkansas to enforce the Supreme Court's decision on Negro integration. In 1958, he sent marines into Lebanon, at the Lebanese government's request, to protect it under the Eisenhower Doctrine of maintaining peace in the Middle East. In December 1958, the United States, Great Britain, and France rejected Soviet demands for the withdrawal of Western troops from West Berlin and for the liquidation of the 4-power occupation of West Berlin.

During Eisenhower's first term the

*(3) COMMANDER OF NATO.*

*(4) G.O.P. NOMINEE.*

195

*General Douglas MacArthur, Chief of Staff, with his aide, Colonel Eisenhower, in Washington in 1931.*

*VICTORY TOAST: Generals Mont-gomery, Eisenhower, Zhukov, Tedder celebrate end of war in Europe in 1945.*

atomic-powered submarine, the *Nautilus,* was launched; the first hydrogen bomb was tested at Eniwetok; the Communist party was declared illegal in the United States. During his second term, the revolt in Hungary was crushed by Soviet troops; Russia launched the *Sputnik;* the United States sent into orbit the first talking satellite which broadcast a recorded Christmas message from President Eisenhower on December 25, 1958. . . .

In the first decade of the Cold War, Eisenhower did all he could to strengthen the nation's defenses. "Only strength can co-operate," he said. "Weakness cannot co-operate: it can only beg." A victorious commander without political ambitions, a soldier who had twice refused to run for the Presidency, General Ike left the White House in March 1961 and retired at seventy to his farm in Gettysburg, Pennsylvania.

*Summary:* EISENHOWER, DWIGHT DAVID. *Born: October 14, 1890 in Denison, Texas. Parents: David Jacob and Ida Stover Eisenhower. Education: West Point, 1915. Married: Mamie Doud in 1916; two children. Career: rose from 2nd Lt. in 1915 to Supreme Commander, Allied Expeditionary Forces in 1943; U.S. Army Chief of Staff, 1945; president, Columbia University, 1948-50; Thirty-fourth President, 1953-61.*

*Presidential candidate at Chicago convention in 1952, with his family.*

*Eisenhower is installed as the 13th President of Columbia University in 1948.*

© Fabian Bachrach

# JOHN F. KENNEDY

*"New Frontiers"*

The first Catholic, first U.S. Navy veteran, first Pulitzer Prize-winning author and the youngest man at forty-three to be elected President, he has demonstrated unusual capacities to meet and overcome great challenges.

Second eldest of nine children, John was a member of a closely-knit but highly competitive family. While he was a student at Choate, his father wrote to him, encouraging him to do better in his studies, "I will not be disappointed if you don't turn out to be a real genius, but I think you can be a really worthwhile citizen with good judgment and good understanding." At Harvard young Kennedy went out for varsity football and swimming. He was overshadowed by his brother Joe who was brilliant both as an athlete and as a student. In 1940 John Kennedy graduated with a Bachelor of Science degree *cum laude*. In 1941 came Pearl Harbor.

At twenty-four, Lt. Kennedy was serving as PT boat commander in the South Pacific. In one dramatic action, shortly after midnight on August 2, 1943, his boat was cut in two by a Japanese destroyer. Kennedy kept his surviving crew of ten afloat in a sea of gasoline; towing one man, he swam five hours to reach a coral reef in the Solomon Islands behind enemy lines. After nine days of extreme privation, he and his crew were rescued through an S O S he had carved

in a coconut shell. Kennedy was awarded the Purple Heart, the Navy and Marine Corps Medal; he was cited by Admiral Halsey for "his courage, endurance, and excellent leadership." In March 1944, he was retired from active duty on account of a back injury he had received.

In 1946 Kennedy was elected to Congress as representative from Massachusetts. In 1952 he won his hard-fought campaign against the incumbent Senator, Henry Cabot Lodge, whose re-election was considered a certainty. Earlier the same year, at a dinner party in Washington, Kennedy had met Jacqueline Lee Bouvier, a twenty-two-year-old beauty. "I leaned across the asparagus and asked

*THE KENNEDY FAMILY* (circa 1937): *a close-knit, happy clan.*

her for a date," Kennedy said later. "It was a spasmodic courtship," Jacqueline recalled. "We didn't see each other for six months. I went to Europe. Jack began his campaigning in Massachusetts." They were married in Newport the next year. In 1956, Kennedy published his *Profiles in Courage,* a study of noble nonconformists in American history. Among other awards, the book won the Pulitzer Prize for biography. Before he reached forty, Kennedy received honorary doctorates from twenty universities. In 1956, he received the "Outstanding Statesman of the Year" Award from the University of Notre Dame; the "Outstanding Irish Catholic in America" Medal from the

*Lt. John Kennedy as PT boat commander in the South Pacific.*

Eire Society; the "Annual Brotherhood Award" from the National Conference of Christians and Jews.

The Presidential race in 1960 was highlighted by a series of four television debates between Senator Kennedy and the Republican candidate, Vice-President Richard Nixon. Not since the Lincoln-Douglas debates a century earlier had a political duel attracted such interest. The two rivals were heard and seen by an audience of seventy million. The debates, which concerned the problem of Cuba and U.S. prestige abroad, did much to make Kennedy a nationally known figure; they helped secure his election in one of the closest races on record.

*In 1946, Kennedy starts his political career, running for a seat in Congress.*

*In 1956, he is one of the Democratic nominees for Vice-President.*

*In 1960, addressing one of the many rallies and meetings in New York City . . . Kennedy campaigned vigorously, entering and winning seven state primaries.*

At his inaugural in 1961 President Kennedy spoke in memorable terms of the challenges which face the world. He urged the Soviet Union and the United States, "to begin anew the quest for peace before the dark powers of destruction unleashed by science engulf all humanity in planned or accidental self-destruction. . . . Let both sides, for the first time, formulate serious and precise proposals for the inspection and control of arms and bring the absolute power to destroy other nations under the absolute control of all nations.

"Let both sides seek to invoke the wonders of science instead of its terrors. Together let us explore the stars, conquer the deserts, eradicate disease, tap the ocean depths, encourage the arts and commerce. . . . My fellow citizens of the world: ask not what America can do for you, but what together we can do for the freedom of man."

*Summary:* KENNEDY, JOHN FITZGERALD. *Born: May 29, 1917 in Brookline, Massachusetts. Parents: Joseph P. and Rose Fitzgerald Kennedy. Education: Harvard, 1940. Married: Jacqueline Lee Bouvier in 1953; two children. Career: U.S. Navy; author; U.S. Representative, 1946-52; U.S. Senator, 1952-60; Thirty-fifth President, 1961-*

*VIENNA MEETING: 1961. President Kennedy, Mrs. Khrushchev; Austrian President Adolf Schaerf; Soviet Premier Khrushchev and Mrs. Kennedy.*

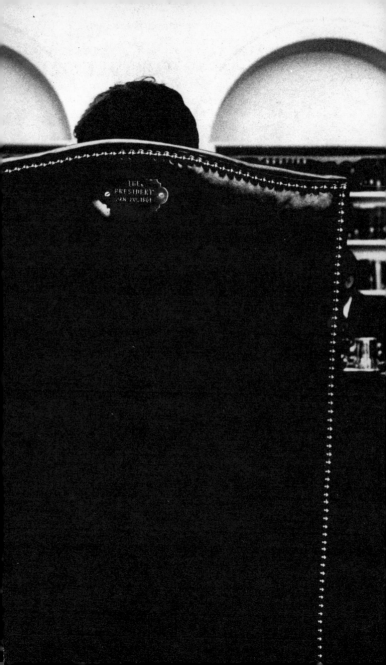

# PRESIDENTIAL

| President | Year of Election | Age at Inaugural | Vice President |
|---|---|---|---|
| 1. George Washington | 1789 | 57 | John Adams |
| George Washington (F) | 1792 | 61 | John Adams |
| 2. John Adams (F) | 1796 | 61 | Thomas Jefferson |
| 3. Thomas Jefferson (DR) | 1800 | 57 | Aaron Burr |
| Thomas Jefferson (DR) | 1804 | 61 | Charles Pinckney |
| 4. James Madison (DR) | 1808 | 57 | George Clinton |
| James Madison (DR) | 1812 | 61 | Elbridge Gerry |
| 5. James Monroe (DR) | 1816 | 58 | Daniel D. Tompkins |
| James Monroe (DR) | 1820 | 62 | Daniel D. Tompkins |
| 6. John Quincy Adams (NR) | 1824 | 57 | John C. Calhoun |

*In the House, Clay threw his electoral votes to Adams.

| President | Year of Election | Age at Inaugural | Vice President |
|---|---|---|---|
| 7. Andrew Jackson (D) | 1828 | 61 | John C. Calhoun |
| Andrew Jackson (D) | 1832 | 65 | Martin Van Buren |
| 8. Martin Van Buren (D) | 1836 | 54 | Richard M. Johnson |
| 9. William Henry Harrison (W) | 1840 | 68 | John Tyler |
| 10. John Tyler (W) | Succeeded to Presidency when | | |
| 11. James Knox Polk (D) | 1844 | 49 | George M. Dallas |
| 12. Zachary Taylor (W) | 1848 | 64 | Millard Fillmore |
| 13. Millard Fillmore (W) | Succeeded to Presidency when | | |
| 14. Franklin Pierce (D) | 1852 | 48 | William R. King |
| 15. James Buchanan (D) | 1856 | 65 | John C. Breckenridge |
| 16. Abraham Lincoln (R) | 1860 | 52 | Hannibal Hamlin |
| Abraham Lincoln (R) | 1864 | 56 | Andrew Johnson |
| 17. Andrew Johnson (R) | Succeeded to Presidency on | | |
| 18. Ulysses Simpson Grant (R) | 1868 | 46 | Schuyler Colfax |
| Ulysses Simpson Grant (R) | 1872 | 50 | Henry Wilson |
| 19. Rutherford Birchard Hayes (R) | 1876 | 54 | William A. Wheeler |
| 20. James Abram Garfield (R) | 1880 | 49 | Chester A. Arthur |
| 21. Chester Alan Arthur (R) | Succeeded to Presidency on | | |

# ELECTIONS 1789-1960

| Popular Vote | Electoral Vote | Defeated Candidates | Popular Vote | Electoral Vote |
|---|---|---|---|---|
| Unknown | 69 | No opponent | Unknown | Unknown |
| Unknown | 132 | No opponent | Unknown | Unknown |
| Unknown | 71 | Thomas Jefferson (DR) | Unknown | 68 |
| Unknown | 73 | Aaron Burr (DR) | Unknown | 73 |
| Unknown | 162 | Charles Pinckney (F) | Unknown | 14 |
| Unknown | 122 | Charles Pinckney (F) | Unknown | 47 |
| Unknown | 128 | DeWitt Clinton (F) | Unknown | 89 |
| Unknown | 183 | Rufus King (F) | Unknown | 34 |
| Unknown | 231 | John Quincy Adams (DR) | Unknown | 1 |
| 108,740 | 84 | Andrew Jackson (D) | 153,544 | 99* |
|  |  | Henry Clay (DR) | 47,136 | 37 |
|  |  | William H. Crawford (DR) | 46,618 | 41 |
| 647,286 | 178 | John Quincy Adams (NR) | 508,064 | 83 |
| 687,502 | 219 | Henry Clay (DR) | 530,189 | 49 |
| 762,678 | 170 | William Henry Harrison (W) | 548,007 | 73 |
| 1,275,016 | 234 | Martin Van Buren (D) | 1,129,102 | 60 |
| Harrison died of pneumonia April 4, 1841 | | | | |
| 1,337,243 | 170 | Henry Clay (W) | 1,299,062 | 105 |
| 1,360,099 | 163 | Lewis Cass (D) | 1,220,544 | 127 |
| Taylor died, July 9, 1850. | | | | |
| 1,601,274 | 254 | Winfield Scott (W) | 1,386,580 | 42 |
| 1,838,169 | 174 | John C. Fremont (R) | 1,341,264 | 114 |
| 1,866,452 | 180 | Stephen A. Douglas (D) | 1,375,157 | 12 |
|  |  | John C. Breckenridge (D) | 847,935 | 72 |
| 2,213,665 | 212 | George B. McClellan (D) | 1,805,237 | 21 |
| Lincoln's assassination, April 15, 1865. | | | | |
| 3,012,833 | 214 | Horatio Seymour (D) | 2,703,249 | 80 |
| 3,597,132 | 286 | Horace Greeley (D) | 2,834,125 | 66 |
| 4,036,298 | 185 | Samuel J. Tilden (D) | 4,300,590 | 184 |
| 4,454,416 | 214 | Winfield S. Hancock (D) | 4,444,952 | 155 |
| Garfield's assassination, September 19, 1881 | | | | |

# PRESIDENTIAL

| President | Year of Election | Age at Inaugural | Vice President |
|---|---|---|---|
| 22. Grover Cleveland (D) | 1884 | 47 | Thomas A. Hendricks |
| 23. Benjamin Harrison (R) | 1888 | 55 | Levi P. Morton |
| 24. Grover Cleveland (D) | 1892 | 55 | Adlai E. Stevenson |
| 25. William McKinley (R) | 1896 | 54 | Garrett A. Hobart |
| William McKinley (R) | 1900 | 60 | Theodore Roosevelt |
| 26. Theodore Roosevelt (R) | Succeeded to Presidency on | | |
| Theodore Roosevelt (R) | 1904 | 46 | Charles W. Fairbanks |
| 27. William Howard Taft (R) | 1908 | 51 | James S. Sherman |
| 28. Woodrow Wilson (D) | 1912 | 56 | Thomas R. Marshall |
| Woodrow Wilson (D) | 1916 | 60 | Thomas R. Marshall |
| 29. Warren Gamaliel Harding (R) | 1920 | 55 | Calvin Coolidge |
| 30. Calvin Coolidge (R) | Succeeded to Presidency when | | |
| Calvin Coolidge (R) | 1924 | 53 | Charles G. Dawes |
| 31. Herbert Hoover (R) | 1928 | 54 | Charles Curtis |
| 32. Franklin Delano Roosevelt (D) | 1932 | 51 | John Nance Garner |
| Franklin Delano Roosevelt (D) | 1936 | 55 | John Nance Garner |
| Franklin Delano Roosevelt (D) | 1940 | 59 | Henry A. Wallace |
| Franklin Delano Roosevelt (D) | 1944 | 63 | Harry S. Truman |
| 33. Harry S. Truman (D) | Succeeded to Presidency on | | |
| Harry S. Truman (D) | 1948 | 63 | Alben W. Barkley |
| 34. Dwight David Eisenhower (R) | 1952 | 62 | Richard M. Nixon |
| Dwight David Eisenhower (R) | 1956 | 66 | Richard M. Nixon |
| 35. John Fitzgerald Kennedy (D) | 1960 | 43 | Lyndon B. Johnson |

Key to Parties: (F) Federalist; (D) Democrat; (R) Republican; (DR).....
(P) People's; (Pr) Progressive; (SR) State's Rights

# ELECTIONS 1789-1960

| Popular Vote | Electoral Vote | Defeated Candidates | Popular Vote | Electoral Vote |
|---|---|---|---|---|
| 4,874,986 | 219 | James G. Blaine (R) | 4,851,981 | 182 |
| 5,439,853 | 233 | Grover Cleveland (D) | 5,540,309 | 168 |
| 5,556,918 | 277 | Benjamin Harrison (R) | 5,176,108 | 145 |
| | | James Weaver (P) | 1,041,028 | 22 |
| 7,104,779 | 271 | William J. Bryan (D) | 6,502,925 | 176 |
| 7,207,923 | 292 | William J. Bryan (D) | 6,358,133 | 155 |
| McKinley's assassination on September 14, 1901 | | | | |
| 7,623,486 | 336 | Alton B. Parker (D) | 5,077,911 | 140 |
| 7,678,908 | 321 | William J. Bryan (D) | 6,409,104 | 162 |
| 6,293,454 | 435 | Theodore Roosevelt (Pr) | 4,119,538 | 88 |
| | | William H. Taft (R) | 3,484,980 | 8 |
| 9,129,606 | 277 | Charles E. Hughes (R) | 8,538,221 | 254 |
| 16,152,200 | 404 | James M. Cox (D) | 9,147,353 | 127 |
| Harding died, August 2, 1923 | | | | |
| 15,725,016 | 382 | John W. Davis (D) | 8,386,503 | 136 |
| | | William M. LaFollette (Pr) | 4,822,856 | 13 |
| 21,391,381 | 444 | Alfred E. Smith (D) | 15,016,443 | 87 |
| 22,821,857 | 472 | Herbert Hoover (R) | 15,761,841 | 59 |
| 27,751,597 | 523 | Alfred Landon (R) | 16,679,583 | 8 |
| 27,244,160 | 449 | Wendell Willkie (R) | 22,305,198 | 82 |
| 25,602,504 | 432 | Thomas E. Dewey (R) | 22,006,285 | 99 |
| Roosevelt's death, April 12, 1945 | | | | |
| 24,105,695 | 303 | Thomas E. Dewey (R) | 21,969,170 | 189 |
| | | J. Strom Thurmond (SR) | 1,169,021 | 39 |
| | | Henry A. Wallace (Pr) | 1,156,103 | 0 |
| 33,824,351 | 442 | Adlai E. Stevenson (D) | 27,314,987 | 89 |
| 35,581,003 | 457 | Adlai E. Stevenson (D) | 25,738,765 | 73 |
| 34,226,925 | 300 | Richard M. Nixon (R) | 34,108,662 | 223 |

...... Democrat-Republican; (NR) National Republican; (W) Whig;

# ACKNOWLEDGMENTS

For their aid in furnishing pictures for the text of AMERICA'S PRESIDENTS the writer is indebted to Ralph H. Anderson, Cornelius W. Heine, Dennis C. Kurjack, and Mrs. Carol Smith, National Park Service, Department of the Interior; Robert H. Haynes, Harvard College Library; Mrs. Emma N. Papert, Metropolitan Museum of Art; Robert Bride and Arthur Carlson, New York Historical Society; Wilson Duprey and Elizabeth Roth, New York Public Library; Prints and Photographs Division, Library of Congress; Herman Kahn, Franklin D. Roosevelt Library; Pierre Salinger; Paul H. Oehser, Smithsonian Institution. For their cooperation he wishes to thank George and Anita Adams, Connie and Jefferson Broady, Novella Busetti; Jehanne S. Carlson, Margaret Giles, Teresa Lengyel; Robert Morton. For their interest and encouragement he is indebted to Edward Ainsworth, Michelina Buoncore, Albert and Elizabeth Elkus; John Edmunds, Evan Koslow; Bruce Lancaster, William McBride, Jr., Frances Moore; Beryl Sokoloff, Lawrence Turner, Merla and Stephen Zellerbach.

# PICTURE SOURCES

Author's collection; pp. 148, 165, 168-9, 172, 178.

Cornell Capa, Magnum Photos; p. 209.

Culver Service; 43, 57, 64, 68, 69, 73, 75, 81, 83, 85, 114-5, 119, 126-7, 128, 129, 133, 134, 143, 144-5, 149, 153, 155, 156, 157, 158-9, 161.

Franklin D. Roosevelt Library; pp. 175, 176, 179, 180, 181, 182-3, 185.

Harvard College Library; pp. 140-1, 146-7.

Independence National Historical Park Collection; pp. 29, 37.

Library of Congress; pp. 18-9, 24-5, 30, 34, 35, 36, 40-1, 45, 58-9, 62-3, 94, 98, 99, 100, 102-3, 104-5, 107, 109, 111, 112-13, 117, 135.

Metropolitan Museum of Art; pp. 50-1, 53, 61.

National Park Service (Abbie Rowe); p. 21.

New York Historical Society; pp. 17, 22-3, 27, 31, 65, 92, 93, 96, 97, 101, 121.

New York Public Library; pp. 39, 79, 115, 116, 123, 125, 131, 139, 151, 160, 162, 163, 169, 194-5, 198.

United Press International; pp. 171, 177, 184, 188-9, 190, 193, 196-7, 199, 201, 208.

White House Press Secretary; pp. 202, 203, 204, 205.
Wide World Photos; pp. 206-7.

Note: the portraits which open each chapter are the official Bureau of Engraving and Printing Presidential Portraits with the exception of President Kennedy's which was engraved especially for this book from the official photograph.

# ▓ FOR FURTHER READING ▓

Adams, John. *Familiar Letters of John Adams and His Wife.* Boston, 1876.

Adams, John Quincy. *Memoirs.* Philadelphia, 1874-1877.

Agar, Herbert. *The People's Choice.* Boston, 1933.

Bowen, Catherine Drinker. *John Adams and the American Revolution.* Boston, 1950.

Bowers, Claude G. *The Young Jefferson.* Boston, 1945.

Butterfield, Roger. *The American Past.* New York, 1947.

Eisenhower, Dwight D. *Crusade in Europe.* New York, 1952.

Freeman, Douglas S. *George Washington.* New York. 1948-57.

Freidel, Frank. *Franklin D. Roosevelt.* Boston, 1952-56.

Grant, U. S. *Memoirs.* New York, 1886.

Hyman, Sidney. *The American President.* New York, 1954.

Jefferson, Thomas. *Selected Writings.* Washington, 1905.

Kennedy, John F. *Profiles in Courage.* New York, 1956.

Lengyel, Cornel. *Four Days in July.* New York, 1958.

Lincoln, Abraham. *Selected Writings.*

Lorant, Stefan. *The Presidency: A Pictorial History.* New York, 1951.

Malone, Dumas. *Jefferson and His Time.* Boston, 1951.

Milhollen, Hirst D. and Milton Kaplan. *Presidents on Parade.* New York, 1948.

Neustadt, Richard E. *Presidential Power.* New York, 1961.

Padover, Saul. *The Genius of America.* New York, 1960.

Roosevelt, Franklin D. *Fireside Chats.* New York, 1940.

Roosevelt, Theodore. *Winning of the West.* New York, 1898.

Sandburg, Carl. *Abraham Lincoln.* New York, 1926-39.

Schlesinger, Arthur M. Jr. *The Age of Jackson.* New York, 1945.

Schlesinger, Arthur M. Jr. *The Age of Roosevelt.* Boston, 1957-60.

Tocqueville, Alexis de. *Democracy in America.* New York, 1960.

Wilson, Woodrow. *Selected Literary & Political Papers.* New York, 1926.

Washington, George. *Writings.* New York, 1889-1893.